Praise for *Quench Your Own Thirst*

USA Today **bestseller**
Wall Street Journal **Business bestseller**
Publishers Weekly **bestseller**

"Today, Sam Adams, named for one of the fieriest of American revolutionaries, has started a revolution of its own, and Jim Koch is a billionaire—a made-in-America success story he writes about in his new book, *Quench Your Own Thirst: Business Lessons Learned Over a Beer or Two*. He's been called the 'Steve Jobs of beer.'"
—*CBS Sunday Morning*

"His story of starting a brewery when no one started breweries, then building it into a $3 billion company and the template for today's craft beer movement, is worth the cover price for fans of entrepreneurial memoir. But it's inspirational for anyone thinking of putting themselves on a more satisfying career path. The bonus is it's a business book offered in friendly, colorful prose that lives up to the title."
—John Carpenter, *Forbes*

"As he outlines in this very insightful page-turner, [Koch] learned lessons the hard way on sales, marketing, hiring, and company culture, and it was those sometimes painful experiences that eventually led him to the top of the hop heap."
—*Entrepreneur*

"Koch's book is a *Siddhartha* of brewing, a journey of discovery, where the young prince—OK, in his midthirties—a successful-yet-dissatisfied Harvard grad, leaves the secure walls of his consultancy palace, armed only with a nineteenth-century beer recipe."
—Neil Steinberg, *Chicago Sun-Times*

"A fluid and colorful writer, Koch captures the entrepreneurial experience with anecdotes and metaphors that will leave those in the trenches nodding in recognition."　　　　—Leigh Buchanan, *Inc.*

"All this happens on page one of Koch's new memoir, *Quench Your Own Thirst* . . . which covers his massive successes over the past three decades: How he revived his family's 120-year-old recipe and dubbed it Samuel Adams Boston Lager. How The Boston Beer Company, as Koch called the company, was able to go public on the New York Stock Exchange by 1995. And how he was running a billion-dollar enterprise by 2015."　　　　—Aaron Goldfarb, *Esquire*

"Boston Beer helped pave the way for craft beer's meteoric rise in the past few decades, and Koch writes about that experience in his new book."　　　　—Kai Ryssdal, host of NPR's *Marketplace*

"In [Koch's] unconventional, conversational new book . . . the man who was among the founding fathers of the craft beer renaissance is unabashedly down to earth and even ribald when it comes to telling his story."　　　　—Bob Townsend,
The Atlanta Journal-Constitution

"The landscape of American beer looked a lot different in the early '80s. Before there were double IPAs and barrel-aged stouts flowing from taps at breweries seemingly on every block, there was one brewery going toe-to-toe with the big dogs. Jim Koch took The Boston Beer Company from scrappy little startup to respected powerhouse over the course of his career, and whether you reach for a Sam Adams or not when you want a beer, you have to respect the man. How did it all happen? How can you steal a little of Koch's business smarts? Read *Quench Your Own Thirst: Business Lessons Learned Over a Beer or Two*."　　　　—Mike Newman, *Cool Material*

"Always true to himself, the author's belief in Samuel Adams and the people around him is what makes his story and philosophy so genuine and endearing. Koch's down-to-earth personality, business advice, and passion are good models for those interested in making their own ways."   —*Kirkus Reviews*

"This is an engaging and well-written blend of stories from a beloved company's founding and sound guidance on surmounting common dilemmas faced in business and in life."   —*Publishers Weekly*

"Jim Koch's new memoir makes him seem like the kind of guy any entrepreneur or investor would want to hang out with at a bar. [Koch] writes about building and running a company in a fun and folksy tone. He is also refreshingly candid about the hard battles and missteps along the way. Unlike many turgid, self-told business books, *Quench Your Own Thirst* goes down easy."   —Reuters

"*Quench Your Own Thirst* is a frosty mug full of sound advice for turning passion into a great business."   —Tony Hsieh

"*Quench Your Own Thirst* introduces an engaging, down-to-earth, fifth-generation brewmaster who also happens to be a savvy, creative, disciplined business mastermind. Jim Koch's story of how he built his beer company—and, incidentally, helped start a new industry in craft beer—serves candid, inspiring insights useful for entrepreneurs in any field. Koch's practical optimism sets the standard for how business success and personal happiness can be beautifully connected."
—Rosabeth Moss Kanter, Harvard Business School
professor and bestselling author of *Confidence:
How Winning Streaks and Losing Streaks Begin
and End* and *Move: How to Rebuild and
Reinvent America's Infrastructure*

"Jim Koch has opened a lot of doors for craft breweries like mine that have succeeded based on the premise of challenging the status quo. Every entrepreneur and aspiring entrepreneur will find useful and sage advice between the covers of *Quench Your Own Thirst*—and Jim's personality, wisdom, and sense of humor come through in his writing as crystal clear as a pint of Sam Adams Lager."　　　—Sam Calagione, president and founder of Dogfish Head Craft Brewery

"Like Steve Jobs, Bill Gates, Larry Ellison, and the other greats, Jim Koch's entrepreneurial journey is motivated by a deep commitment to making superb products and building a unique culture that reinforces innovation and risk-taking. This book tells a compelling story about how he did it. The lessons will be invaluable for anyone starting a business or building a career."　　　—Bill Hambrecht, cofounder of Hambrecht & Quist and chairman of WR Hambrecht + Co

"Anyone enjoying America's current Golden Age of Beer will be fascinated by Jim Koch's story of how it came to be. But this is really a book about the individual and team traits necessary to build any enterprise—and about the paradoxical combination of hardheaded practicality, impractical dreaming, long-term vision, and minute-by-minute adaptability required for success. Jim Koch once called Samuel Adams beer 'America's classic lager.' He has written a classic American story of pluck, ingenuity, setbacks, and achievement, all in a tone of gently self-mocking humor."　　　—James Fallows, national correspondent for *The Atlantic*

"For me, Sam Adams was not only the best beer I've ever tasted but also the best investment I ever made."　　　—John Paulson, founder of Paulson & Co.

QUENCH
YOUR OWN
THIRST

BUSINESS LESSONS LEARNED

OVER A BEER OR TWO

JIM KOCH

FLATIRON
BOOKS
NEW YORK

For Cynthia, sine qua non.

For John, my dear lost friend.

And for my father and mother, my first and best teachers.

The author would like to note that in most cases where he has defaulted to a masculine pronoun, a feminine pronoun would also work just as well.

QUENCH YOUR OWN THIRST. Copyright © 2016 by Jim Koch. All rights reserved. Printed in the United States of America. For information, address Flatiron Books, 175 Fifth Avenue, New York, N.Y. 10010.

www.flatironbooks.com

The Library of Congress has cataloged the hardcover edition as follows:

Names: Koch, James, 1949– author.
Title: Quench your own thirst : business lessons learned over a beer or two / Jim Koch.
Description: First edition. | New York : Flatiron Books, [2016]
Identifiers: LCCN 2015046334 | ISBN 978-1-250-07050-0 (hardcover) |
    ISBN 978-1-250-07051-7 (e-book)
Subjects: LCSH: Koch, James, 1949– | Boston Beer Company. | Beer industry—United
    States—Management. | Entrepreneurship. | BISAC: BUSINESS & ECONOMICS /
    Entrepreneurship.
Classification: LCC HD9397.U54 B675 2016 | DDC 658—dc23
LC record available at http://lccn.loc.gov/2015046334

ISBN 978-1-250-13501-8 (trade paperback)

Our books may be purchased in bulk for promotional, educational, or business use. Please contact your local bookseller or the Macmillan Corporate and Premium Sales Department at 1-800-221-7945, extension 5442, or by email at MacmillanSpecialMarkets@macmillan.com

First Flatiron Books Paperback Edition: September 2017

10 9 8 7 6 5 4 3 2 1

CONTENTS

Introduction   *1*

PART I: MASHING

1. Blow It Up   9

2. Turn Your Receiver On   14

3. Open Yourself to "Holy Shit"   18

4. Make It Better or Cheaper   22

5. Do the Math   24

6. Avoid "Smart" Investors   25

7. Look Hard for Talent. Then Look Again   29

8. The Best Marketing Plan Ever   32

9. Find Your Yoda   35

10. Sacred Cod Boston Lager?   43

11. The Difference Between Sex and Masturbation   49

CONTENTS

PART II: BOILING AND COOLING

12. String Theory 53

13. "I Make My Money When I Buy the Goods" 64

14. The Strength of the Weak 66

15. The Golden Rule of Selling 72

16. My Best Sales Call of All Time 75

17. You Can't Hear with Someone Else's Ears 78

18. You Don't Climb a Mountain to Get to the Middle 86

19. Give Them Something to Talk About 89

20. When You're Right, Push It 95

21. Take the Giant Turds in Stride 101

PART III: FERMENTING

22. Grow Skinny 109

23. If You're Not the Lead Dog, the Scenery
Never Changes 115

24. Launch Your Long Shots 120

25. There's No Pretending About Quality 126

26. The Most Expensive Education You'll Ever Get 130

27. We Take Beer Seriously, but Not Ourselves 137

28. The CEO Flies Coach 141

29. The "Fuck You" Rule 144

30. Always Raise the Average 149

31. Make Your Public Offering Public 156

32. Learn to Take a Punch 164

PART IV: MATURATION

33. Grow When You're Not Growing   175

34. Endure the Endings   186

35. Mind Your Protection   192

36. If the Sun Is Shining, Look Out for an Avalanche   198

37. The Recall: Our Best Crisis Ever   205

38. Let Helga Do the Talking   210

PART V: PACKAGING

39. Practice *Fingerspitzengefühl*   219

40. Stop Painting and Start Partnering   225

41. Welcome the Dude with the Gold-Painted Toenails   230

42. Quench Your Own Thirst   238

Acknowledgments   *241*

Jim's Bookshelf   *245*

Notes   *251*

Index   *253*

INTRODUCTION

From the way my father was looking at me, you'd think I had just proposed robbing a bank. A big, ominous-looking bank with gun-toting security guards. "Why in the world would you do *that*?" he asked.

"Uh, well—"

He waved his finger at me. "You'll never succeed. The big guys will eat you alive. They'll grind you up like they did me." He shook his head. "It's taken our family a hundred and fifty years to get the smell of the brewery out of our clothes."

We were sitting in my parents' kitchen in Cincinnati. Picture a 1950s linoleum floor, Formica counters, and wallpaper depicting culinary dishes in alphabetical order, apple strudel to zucchini bread. It was the spring of 1984, and I had just announced that at the age of thirty-four, I was quitting my job as a management consultant to start a beer company. I figured my dad would be happy. After all, he had been a brewmaster. *His* father had also been a brewmaster. So had *his* father. And *his* father. Five generations of first sons in the Koch family had brewed beer, making us the longest line of brewmasters in the

United States. And now, with me, the lineage would continue. What could be better?

I pointed to the business plan I had spread out on the kitchen table. "Dad, nobody's doing this the right way. I think I've got a way to make a go of it." I sketched out my idea to start a small-scale beer company in Boston making high-quality beer for a limited number of drinkers in the region. "I'm not going to compete with the big boys like Anheuser-Busch. I know they'd kill me. But there's another way. I'm going to look for drinkers who appreciate good beer and who would pay a premium for richer, more flavorful beer. I'm sure those drinkers exist. If I just focus on making a better beer, I know *somebody* will drink it."

Dad tapped the table impatiently, although I thought he seemed at least faintly interested now. "Are there enough of these drinkers? Can you make a living?"

"Not the living I currently make, but I can make a living." I pointed at some numbers I'd calculated. "I think after five years I'll make five thousand barrels a year, with eight employees and $1.2 million in revenue. That's enough."

"That's not much."

"No, but it's enough. And I'll be happy. I'll be running my own small brewery."

My father thought about this for a moment. "It's not realistic. Brewing today is about size—nothing else. You're crazy!"

"Dad, there *are* a few microbreweries that have started up." In fact, there were about a dozen, mostly on the West Coast. Quality was unpredictable. Cracking open a bottle, you didn't know whether you would get a really great beer or a science project.

"How many are making any money?" Dad asked.

"Probably none."

He laughed. "Sounds like a good business. You make beer but no money. How long can you afford to do that?"

He was right: There was scant reason to think my venture would be any different. But I was determined to leave my job and start my own business, and brewing was the idea I had come up with that excited me. I wanted to persuade him (and myself) that I wasn't crazy.

We sat there, neither of us speaking. Without warning, he rose to his feet. "Jim, follow me."

"Where are we going?"

"Just follow me."

He led me up to the attic. He flicked on a light and began walking toward the back.

"Why are we up here?"

"I want to show you something."

I followed him, taking care not to bump my head. We made our way around boxes and old furniture until we came to a dusty trunk on which he had stacked years of *Road & Track* and *Motor Trend* magazines. (Other than his family, Charles J. Koch loved two things: cars and beer.) "Here, help me with this." We moved the magazines and cracked open the trunk. Inside were notebooks, folders, and loose papers—some scrawled with handwriting, all yellowed with age. He rifled through papers and held a few up for me to see. "This is what is left of the Koch family beer archives—my course material, my brewing notes." He pulled out a thin folder. "And here are the family recipes." Resting the folder on the edge of the trunk, he opened it and read for a few minutes in silence. Then he let out a little hoot as he shook a piece of paper he'd found. "This is the best beer recipe our family has! It's old—from the 1860s. If you're going to do this crazy thing, you might as well start with the best recipe."

He handed me the paper so I could take a look. Moving to where the light was better, I saw that the recipe was for an "all-malt" beer, one that adhered to the *Reinheitsgebot* (a German beer purity law dating to 1516). The *Reinheitsgebot* was the world's first consumer protection law, stipulating that beer could contain only four ingredients: water, yeast, malted barley or wheat, and hops. Virtually all twentieth-century American beers and some European beers used corn, rice, and preservatives in addition to malt because those ingredients were cheaper and made the beer lighter and "more drinkable." The recipe my father gave me took none of these shortcuts. It made a substantial beer, pure and simple. And it used traditional, nearly forgotten brewing techniques with arcane names like kräusening, decoction mashing, and dry hopping.

I glanced through the recipe and then looked at my father. "You won't be sorry you gave this to me."

He had one thing to add: "Just do me a favor. Make a good beer, and don't worry about the marketing. People drink the beer; they don't drink the marketing. Don't get distracted. Just worry about the beer."

I promised him I would.

THE COMPANY I FOUNDED in 1984, the Boston Beer Company (BBC), gave me both pleasure and purpose beyond my wildest dreams. By 1988, my founding partner, Rhonda Kallman, and I were selling 36,000 barrels a year, seven times what we'd anticipated. Rhonda had been my assistant at Boston Consulting Group (BCG), the management consulting firm where I'd been working, and her skills complemented mine perfectly. Together, we sustained the company's exponential growth for years. We won awards at beer competitions, entered dozens of new markets, added dozens of employees, and began to offend the companies making big imported beers like Heineken, Corona, and Beck's. Other start-ups rushed to replicate our success, and the craft beer segment was born.

In 1995, when Boston Beer went public and began selling shares of its stock on the New York Stock Exchange, it seemed we could do no wrong. And then, just months later, the empire struck back (to use a *Star Wars* metaphor) in the form of an industry Goliath hell-bent on the destruction of Sam Adams in particular and craft beer in general. Everything we had worked for was at risk. We persevered, though, and some twenty years later the craft revolution is stronger than ever, accounting for more than 10 percent of the overall beer market. Driven by further innovations like Angry Orchard hard cider, Boston Beer's 2015 revenues have reached nearly $1 billion. That might be an impressive-sounding number, but Samuel Adams is still only about 1 percent of the overall U.S. beer market. That's right; it took us thirty years to get to 1 percent. We started at invisible, grew to infinitesimal, got to minuscule, and moved to tiny. In 2015 we can proudly say, "We finally made it to small!"

Never in a million years did I think Boston Beer would grow to employ more than a thousand people. Never did I think I'd get to drink some 24,000 beers *as part of my job*. Never did I think my work days would be so diverse and engaging, and that they would include tasting experimental brews, presiding over weddings at our brewery (I've been a bridesmaid on three occasions—always a bridesmaid, never a bride), getting dunked into a tank of expired beer, designing brewing equipment, making yearly trips to Germany to select hops, and having a gun pulled on me by a startled bar owner.

As I've described these experiences in bars across the world, people have asked me what I've learned—what words of wisdom do I have? This book is my answer. I serve up stories I hope will help you if you're starting a new business, working in an established one, or trying to figure out what you want to do next. I address specific business topics like sales, hiring, innovation, culture, and leadership, but I also advocate for a broader approach of openness and experimentation in business and life. And of course, I include discussion of my most colossal screw-ups.

In the spirit of a tavern conversation, I invite you to settle into your favorite chair, crack open a cold Sam, and imagine we are sitting together. Cheers!

PART I

MASHING

(1983-1985)

Combine milled grain with hot water, and you get a thick mixture—a "mash"—that resembles porridge. Heating this mash will break down complex carbohydrates into simpler sugars. The sugars will later be turned into alcohol during the fermentation process. The "magic" of brewing thus doesn't just happen; you need to create the right conditions first by making just the right mash.

1

BLOW IT UP

PEOPLE FREQUENTLY ASK how I could have given up a very good consulting job for a new and uncharted path as a brewer-entrepreneur. I was supporting a wife and two small children at the time; wasn't I scared to blow up my life like that? What if it failed?

Well, there were two sides to it. On the one hand, I liked my job, but I didn't love it, and I was willing to take a risk in order to do something I loved. On the other hand, blowing up my life wasn't as scary as it might seem. Growing up, I watched my dad leave his career as a brewer to start a new one as an entrepreneur. First, he took a sales position with a company that sold brewing chemicals, and then a few years after that he started his own company distributing industrial chemicals. He worked long hours but enjoyed being his own boss, answering only to himself.

Throughout my childhood, my dad's mantra was: *Every problem has a solution.* This optimistic yet pragmatic perspective helped my dad overcome any fears he might have had as he started his own business—and, I might add, it helped him in the rest of his life, too. When my dad was eighty, a hip replacement he'd gotten years before was giving out and walking was becoming extremely painful.

Meanwhile, my mother was suffering from Parkinson's disease, a condition that robbed them of those "golden years" of retirement. It would have been easy for my father to feel powerless and fall into depression. But you know what he told me one day over lunch? He said, "Jim, can you believe this? I'm *eighty*! This is so great. I never thought I'd live to be eighty. Nobody in our family ever has. This is wonderful! I've got so much to be happy about."

As a kid, I watched my dad's pragmatic optimism in action every day. But I didn't just soak it in; I put it into practice myself. When the washing machine broke, Dad and I went down to the cellar with a toolbox, took the thing apart, and figured out what was wrong. When my sister was old enough to drive, Dad and I went out to the garage every night for a month and fixed up his rusty old Ford convertible for her. We filled the body panels with Bondo and fiberglass and sanded down the exterior, taped it, and spray-painted it ourselves. When we wanted to fence in our backyard for the dogs, Dad showed up with a trailer full of fence posts, and we spent the weekend with a posthole digger. "Oh, crap," I remember thinking when I saw that trailer. But we put in five hundred feet of fence, one hole at a time. It lasted twenty-five years.

We enjoyed our share of family activities, but the ones I remember most growing up had to do with work, not play. No job was a "dirty" job; all work was worthwhile and valued as a craft. One year my family and I planted thousands of Christmas trees on our farm. Other times my brother and I went to my dad's company and helped him fill drums of chemicals. (We didn't know it then, but these chemicals, which included aromatic solvents like trichloroethane and perchlorethylene, were carcinogens. But they smelled wonderful.) When I was a teenager, I had a business mowing lawns in the summer and shoveling snow in winter. Another summer, I tarred driveways. I had to wrestle these huge, eight-hundred-pound drums off trucks and squeegee tar into cracks in the asphalt. I was dressed head to toe, even in the summer heat, to keep the tar off my skin.

All these chores and jobs forced me to solve problems, and to rely on my own resources to do it. When obstacles arose, I thought, *Okay, there's a solution out there. Maybe I can't see it, but it exists. I have everything I need inside me to find it. If I try hard and still don't see the answer, then maybe I need to start fresh. Eventually, I will see it. Every problem has a solution.*

By the time I reached my mid-thirties, starting a company didn't seem fundamentally different from any other practical task I'd attempted. I wasn't terrified at the prospect of leaving stability and familiarity behind, because I knew things would work out. Even if the solution to a problem didn't come to me immediately, I knew that if I hung in there, I would find it. I just needed to be in the right frame of mind to see it.

DOING SOMETHING YOU LOVE isn't the only reason to start a new life. You could also do it to *find out* what you love, or to prevent yourself from moving too far down a track you suspect isn't for you.

Starting Boston Beer was actually the *second* time I'd blown up my life. Once before, sensing that I had put myself on the wrong career track, I stopped the train and let myself off.

The year was 1973. I was twenty-four years old, and instead of working toward something I cared about, I had enrolled in graduate school, a dual J.D./M.B.A. program at Harvard. I had gone to Harvard as an undergraduate, and now I felt like I was in "nineteenth grade," sequestered in what was essentially a womb with a view. I was starting to make permanent commitments and choices, but I knew I didn't want to practice law or work in a big company, the two paths my classmates were running down. There must have been other options out there, but I didn't know what they were. How could I have known? I hadn't really done anything in my life but go to school.

I felt trapped, like I was floating down a pounding river. If I continued on toward graduation, I would be routed onto a life stream I didn't want. The only choice was to stop the momentum toward "the rest of my life." So that's what I did. I wrote letters to the deans of Harvard Law School and Harvard Business School, telling them I was dropping out. They urged me to reconsider, since I would have to reapply for admission if I wanted to return. But I had decided. I didn't want to go where the river was taking me.

A friend of mine was working as an instructor at Outward Bound, an intensive outdoor program designed to foster mental toughness. Having fallen in love with hiking, rock climbing, and other outdoor sports in college, and having saved up a little money from manual labor jobs I had been working, I decided to try it for the summer. I accepted an internship at the Colorado school, which turned out to be a great move. Outward Bound gave me a chance to open my mind and see life from a new perspective far away from Harvard. On our expeditions, we didn't live off the land (poisonous plants look pretty much like safe ones, and the animals you can catch and kill often have diseases). Rather, in our forty-pound packs, we carried the stuff we would need: food, fuel, and gear for two weeks until resupply. We were off the grid, totally self-sufficient. Each morning, we got up, looked at the map, and figured out how we were going to get to our next campsite. In the middle of the twenty-eight-day course was the "solo." For three days, each person was completely alone. You had your tarp and sleeping bag, your place where you stayed, six matches, and a dozen saltines. And a notebook. It's an experience most people never have in their entire life. No people, no books, nothing but your own thoughts. The solitude and loneliness of the wilderness was strange at first, but I quickly got used to it. It was a way for me to cast aside the weight of other people's expectations and come to grips with my true self.

The summer went quickly, and eventually I got promoted to full instructor. I got used to not living anywhere, sometimes from one resupply point to another. I found it invigorating to have no real responsibilities except to myself—life was now a blank canvas, every day a new choice.

Over the next three years, I was at Outward Bound schools in the mountains of Colorado, the desert in Texas, the mountains in Oregon, the lakes of Minnesota, and the rivers and mountains of British Columbia. During the winters, I left Outward Bound and spent stretches of time working odd jobs and projects in Cambridge, Seattle, and Cincinnati. Even when I was back in civilization, I spent weekends mountaineering, rock climbing, kayaking, skiing, canoeing, and backpacking. I climbed mostly in the Pacific Northwest, where unclimbed peaks still existed. There were peaks in the North Cascades where I'd say to myself, surveying the panoramic view, *Wow, it's possible that no other human being has ever stood on this spot.*

In retrospect, that's kind of what I was doing with my life—charting my own path. It may have seemed like I was a "dropout," and in a literal sense I was. I was moving in no particular direction, toward no particular goal. To my Harvard classmates, I looked like a loser. But I was also laying the foundation for life as an entrepreneur. I thought of myself as gathering my forces.

Should you change something big in your life? Should you switch departments or take on a new role? Should you quit your job and start a business? I can't tell you that. What I do know is you shouldn't settle when it comes to work and career. If you're going to work hard, you should find it satisfying and meaningful. Work is too much a part of your life and identity *not* to. The right career for you is out there, and it's worth a lot of searching—years, even—to find it. Take some risks; blow it all up if you have to. And start anew. After all, most risks aren't really risky. Isn't the biggest risk of all that you'll waste your life doing what you don't really enjoy doing, making compromise after compromise?

2

TURN YOUR RECEIVER ON

BACK IN 1983, when I started thinking about starting my own business, I had no idea what it would be. It's not like I had always been obsessed with beer. Sure, beer was a fairly strong presence in our family life when I was growing up; I visited breweries with my father on many occasions, and, in keeping with our German heritage, we kids were sometimes given a little beer with dinner. But that didn't translate automatically into an irresistible business idea. When I first thought of leaving my job at Boston Consulting Group, I was more attuned to what I *didn't* want out of a job. I loved the intellectual challenge of consulting, but the constant business travel had gotten to me. I wanted to see more of my family while doing something I enjoyed, something that was meaningful.

Somehow, being in the position of not knowing exactly what kind of business to start didn't cause me to freak out. Instead, I tuned in. At BCG, I had traveled around the country helping industrial companies solve strategic problems in their foundries, paper mills, and factories. I was so busy focusing on the job every day, week, and month that I didn't think about possible ideas for starting my own business. Why would I? Entrepreneurs weren't high profile back in 1983. Successful entrepreneurs in Boston worked mostly in the high-tech industry, which didn't appeal to me. And entrepreneurship didn't have the cachet it enjoys today (this was pre–Internet revolution and pre–Steve Jobs ruling the universe). For a young professional with a good education, starting a business seemed eccentric and a little peculiar. Most people just aspired to a good job in a big company.

Once I decided that I wanted to start my own company, ideas started popping up out of nowhere. Business ideas are like radio signals. They're out there, and, in fact, they surround us. The trick is to turn your receiver on so you can tune in. Once my receiver was turned on, I was almost overwhelmed with possibilities, opportunities, and ideas.

One idea I had was to start a business putting private telephone branch exchanges into apartment buildings. Back then, a building with thirty apartments had at least thirty landlines coming into it. You paid for each of them but you didn't need all of them, because a relatively small percentage of residents were on the phone at any given time. If you figured out the usage patterns, you could put in a switch and those thirty condos could share, say, ten lines at a third of the cost.

I'm glad I didn't pursue that idea. Drastic changes in the telecommunications industry made it obsolete ten years later. Who has landlines anymore? Another idea I had was to create small, stand-alone emergency rooms—what is now called a "doc-in-a-box." It's very expensive to treat people in traditional emergency rooms. Hospital ERs are inefficient because you have to be prepared to treat all patients—kids with colds alongside people with life-threatening catastrophes. If your emergency isn't life threatening, you can sit for hours in a germy waiting room. I thought I could staff and equip a small emergency room at half the price of a conventional one. But, as with the landline idea, I researched this one, talked about it with others, and concluded that I couldn't make it work. (Since then, others have found a business model that *does* work. Every problem has a solution.)

One day in the winter of 1983, about a year before I told my dad my plans and he gave me the family recipe, my dad handed me an *Inc.* magazine article about Fritz Maytag (of the washing machine family). Maytag had spent a lot of family money resurrecting the defunct Anchor Brewing Company and putting out a craft beer called Anchor Steam. Fritz later told me about his experience with small-scale brewing in a memorable quote: "If you want to make a small fortune brewing beer, start with a large fortune."

My dad wasn't trying to spark an idea in me; he just thought the article was interesting and a little weird. Yet it caught my imagination. *Huh,* I thought, *I don't have Fritz Maytag's family fortune, but maybe there's another way to start a brewery. There is nothing like Anchor Steam in Boston. Maybe I can tap a market, however small, for good beer.* I had been home brewing off and on for a few years, seeing it as a way to feel connected to my family's heritage (President Jimmy Carter had only legalized home brewing in 1978 and it hadn't yet become popular). I understood the basics and, having worked with manufacturing processes at the consulting company, I also thought I had a basic understanding of what was required to brew great beer consistently and on a commercial scale.

I realized that I would face several challenges in getting this business off the ground. First, I would have to persuade drinkers to pay a premium for a beer that was richer and more flavorful than the pale, bland beers that were then as ubiquitous as Coke and Pepsi. I would also need to change the minds of drinkers who preferred imports, teaching them that the skunky aroma and cardboard taste they thought they liked were really just signs of stale beer. (The green or clear bottles favored by imports allowed light to get in, promoting a reaction with oxygen called oxidation. Fusel alcohols, acetaldehyde, trans-2-nonenal, and other molecules that produced a stale, cardboard flavor.)

Next, I would need to demonstrate something far more difficult: that an American brewer could brew beer that was as good as or better than the pricey European brews. Despite the imports' skunky taste, beer drinkers assumed that if a beer came from Germany or Belgium or even Canada or Mexico, it had to be better than American beer. And they were probably right: Virtually all American beer *was* watery, fizzy, and inexpensive. Yet America had once made many big, flavorful beers. We had a much more distinguished brewing tradition than people realized. It was time to help people rediscover that.

If I could overcome all of these hurdles in educating drinkers, then the real Beer 101 would start. I would need to teach drinkers about the importance of brown bottles over green (to protect the beer from the damaging effects of light), about the reliable freshness of our product, and about quality ingredients and brewing practices. If I could teach drinkers *all* that, then, I thought, they would seek out a beer brewed in America using the world's best ingredients and packaged to protect the integrity of the beer.

My idea boiled down (no pun intended) to three basic phases: Make great beer. Give it to people fresh. Find customers.

Thus was born the simple business idea that has sustained me for the past thirty years. I had turned my receiver on, but I needed to switch the channels a few times before I found a tune I liked. If you like the thought of being your own boss, don't stress out about finding the "perfect" company to start. Listen—and listen some more. When you happen upon the right channel, you'll know it.

OPEN YOURSELF TO "HOLY SHIT"

REALITY IS NOTHING BUT A COLLECTIVE HUNCH.
—LILY TOMLIN

OF COURSE, IT'S POSSIBLE to listen and not hear. How open are you to truly path-breaking ideas? Do you find the status quo unsatisfying or annoying? Are you willing to start a business that overturns that status quo?

I was, and I owe part of that to something I learned in college. Everyone was required to take at least one science course. I found one that didn't require any real math or science and that was taught by several professors, including James Watson, who had recently won the Nobel Prize for codiscovering DNA. I knew I was going to be okay in the course when Professor Watson kept writing on the blackboard the name of creatures he was studying—"fruit flys [*sic*]." He may have won the Nobel Prize, but I could spell better.

Spelling aside, Watson and the other professors did manage to teach me something. The course was about scientific revolutions, times when the way we understood the world changed drastically. Astronomers used to believe that all heavenly bodies circled the earth, but they eventually came to believe that the earth in fact circled the sun while spinning on its axis. Likewise, scientists initially believed that combustion originated in combustible material called phlogiston. Then they discovered that oxygen was the mechanism by which fire was made. When I read Thomas Kuhn's writings on such "paradigm shifts," it struck me that we only *think* we know what we know, and that most of our assumptions at any point in time are wrong and will be revised.

We build all these frameworks, models, and modes of understanding to organize and *explain* what we experience. But there are always discrepancies or inexplicable truths, if you will, that fall outside our models. Our knee-jerk response? Either ignore these inexplicable truths or explain them away inelegantly. The Ptolemaic theory of the earth as the center of the universe (with other planets and the sun orbiting around it) made sense to astronomers for two thousand years. Some celestial movements didn't fit into the theory of bodies circling the earth. So astronomers created exceptions to the theory, what was known as "retrograde motion," to account for these unusual movements. It worked imperfectly, but well enough as a theory of the heavens. Ultimately, though, it was replaced by Copernican astronomy, with its notion of the planets revolving around the sun. Of course, nothing in the natural world changed. The planets still moved exactly as before. We were just explaining what we observed differently.

Kuhn's thinking holds clear relevance for business. Most commercial activity operates within the accepted paradigms of how the world works, with companies making incremental improvements in cost or quality. Entire industries are built around expanding and tweaking the accepted paradigm, and attempts to challenge the accepted paradigm are almost always frowned upon or marginalized, dismissed as impractical or wrongheaded. The truth is that *most of the value in an industry is created precisely by people who venture outside of conventional wisdom.* You know the people I'm talking about—the ones who embrace those wondrously creative, "holy shit" moments and who go on to do what most people didn't expect or even think was possible.

Here's an example: During the 1980s, the best-selling drug in the world was Tagamet, a billion-dollar-a-year blockbuster that treated stomach ulcers by inhibiting the acid production that was "proven" to cause them. Then a thirty-one-year-old doctor in Perth, Australia, and his research partner came along with a crazy theory that Tagamet was essentially useless; ulcers, these doctors claimed, were not caused by stomach acid at all but by weird bacteria. Conventional wisdom held that no bacteria could live in the highly acidic environment of a stomach. Well, it turned out there *was* such a bacterium. Established medical experts didn't believe it. The Australian doctor proved his theory by drinking a beaker of the bacteria, developing stomach ulcers ten days later, and then curing himself of the ulcers with common antibiotics within two weeks. Holy shit! Who would have thought that? I'll tell you who: an outsider operating in relative obscurity beyond his field's established authorities and institutions. This outsider, I might add, won the Nobel Prize in 2005.

As a management consultant, I always took a special interest in the outliers in any industry. We would draw graphs to prove general rules, like the bigger the company, the larger the profits, or the faster the equipment ran, the lower the cost—stuff like that. But in processing the data, we always had certain data points that were off the line. Most people looked at the graph and saw the general rule, but I liked to observe and wonder at the weirdness of the outliers. Everybody already knew the general rule—that's why it was the general rule. For me, the real opportunity lay in understanding the outliers, since these phenomena reflected activity that people usually ignored.

In the beer business, the general rule during the 1980s was clear: The economics of scale in marketing, production, and sales made it impossible for small businesses to compete. In that context, Anchor Steam emerged as an outlier from which to learn. Why did it survive even though the general rule held true? The answer was that it wasn't competing with the big brewers. Anchor Steam was making more flavorful beer and charging a premium.

As you tune in to listen for your great business idea, don't get too influenced by what most people in an industry or a field say you "need to do." Go your own way. A new business is built on a different and better approach than what's already out there. And it's okay to enter a field you know only a little about, because that little bit that you know can be key. Ignorance can actually be a huge asset, giving you the *best* vantage point. When I started The Boston Beer Company, I had no serious beer industry experience on my side—only ignorance and Thomas Kuhn. But that was a lot.

You'll of course want to look for skeptics who can help you test your idea. Some entrepreneurs fall so in love with their genius concept that they think they can't lose. I get worried when I hear "all my friends love it." Friends aren't the same as real-life customers who are being asked to fork over their hard-earned money. What your friends should be alerting you to, if they are to be of any use, is not how great the idea is, but all the obstacles you will have to overcome—and how you might begin to overcome them.

Truly historic "holy shit" moments don't happen to everyone. Still, you never know. Ideas that, at first glance, may seem quirky, strange, or unorthodox are sometimes the only ones that will work. Revolutions do happen. Maybe not all at once, but in time and with patience and perseverance on the part of the revolutionaries. If we're too certain, too stuck in our ways, too invested in "the way things are done," we run the risk of missing out on all the fun of creating a better world, or at least one with better beer.

4

MAKE IT BETTER OR CHEAPER

NOT LONG AGO, *Harvard Business Review* published an article on a two-decade-long study of thousands of businesses. The research revealed that there were precisely two rules of successful companies. The first rule: You succeed by adding value rather than reducing cost. The second: There are no other rules. I would add a third: If you can do both, you have a home run.

Let's break this down a bit. Value is a function of two things: not just the quality of a product, but also its price. Value *for the money*. It follows that any enterprise can compete in a market by either selling better products than its peers or by selling products at a lower price . . . or both. But if you don't do one of those two things, then you don't have a business, and you aren't going to stay around long. Therefore, my mantra for crafting a business plan is simple: Make your product better or cheaper.

Which of these strategic routes—quality or price—should you choose? The first business challenge I worked on as a BCG consultant involved a foundry that was making castings (that is, parts "cast" by pouring molten metal into a mold) for car transmissions. Our casting was a little more expensive than the competition's—say, something like $2.70 per casting as opposed to $2.50. Yet ours had a lower failure rate and therefore was higher quality. When you factored in the $1,000 that car companies would pay to replace a damaged transmission because a casting failed, the failure rate became extremely important. Also, our castings were more uniform, so our customers didn't have to reset the machining line (an expensive proposition) when one of them came in slightly off-spec. Our castings weren't the lowest price, but they gave our customers the *lowest total cost*. So in this case, our product was better *and* cheaper overall. We sold millions of them.

It seemed like this foundry was competing on price, but really quality played the pivotal role. I came away from this assignment and others like it realizing that it is *far* more attractive for a company to offer better quality than a lower price. Price is important, but if that's all you have to offer customers, then eventually you're just a commodity and you hit a dead end in the market. You're stuck always trying to be the lowest-price provider, cutting corners to reduce your costs. Somebody can always underprice you by cutting more corners. It seems much more interesting, creative, and profitable to focus on *adding* value by upping product quality rather than just trying to do what others have already done, just a little cheaper.

As I began to think about starting my own company, I was determined that any enterprise I created would clear a place for itself in the market by doing something *better* than its competition. That's where all the passion and excitement in business was. We wouldn't just ask customers to pay more; we would give them a good reason for doing so. In crafting your business plan, be brutally honest: Are you really providing a better product or service than what's out there? Does anyone truly care? If so, can you do it at a price point that enough customers will find palatable? If not, is there another business you're excited about that *would* allow you to do something better?

Better or cheaper, there's no way around it. Make it one of these, or don't make it at all.

5

DO THE MATH

DURING THOSE YEARS at BCG, people often approached me with ideas for new products or businesses and asked what I thought. At first I would try to analyze the opportunity with complicated tools, everything from conjoint analysis to logarithmic price-volume relationships. The analysis not only gave me headaches; it also wasn't very useful.

After figuring out the "better or cheaper" principle, I recognized an important corollary: The size of your business is defined by the number of customers who care about getting either the higher quality or the lower cost, as well as by how much these customers purchase.

Once you've figured these things out, you have a simple and quick way to determine the viability of a business. The number of customers times the average number of units they will purchase times the price they will pay for these purchases yields your revenues. The cost per unit at the projected volume gives you your variable costs, which is subtracted from the revenues to get your gross margin dollars. If that number is bigger than your fixed costs, you're making money and can grow. If it's not bigger on an ongoing basis, you don't have a business. In many years of advising small businesses, I've been constantly amazed at how often people fail to do this simple calculation.

6

AVOID "SMART" INVESTORS

I INCORPORATED BOSTON BEER Company on July 2, 1984. My first important task, one that only took a few weeks, was to secure funding. I calculated that I needed $250,000 to start the company. I had taken out a second mortgage to cover my daily living expenses until I could afford to pay myself, which I anticipated would be about a year later. I thought I wouldn't be able to rent good office or warehouse space, but as it turned out, I managed to find a place that really spoke to me. I signed a one-year lease for $80 a month for warehouse space in the old Haffenreffer Brewery, which had been the last operating brewery in the city of Boston. Since the brewery's closure in the mid-1960s, the building had fallen into disrepair and had been largely abandoned. More recently, a neighborhood group had taken it over with the hope of renovating it. In 1984, it was still very much a work in progress.

The brewery complex comprised a jumble of red brick buildings from the nineteenth century, complete with an old stable building, a brick smokestack, and a few corrugated sheds. Some of the buildings had gaping holes in the ceiling; the main building even had trees growing out of the front wall. There were a few paying tenants, including a guy I called Pablo the Porno Painter because of his style and subject matter. You get the gist. A few squatters had taken up residence in the complex. The nonprofit community group that owned the complex decided it was more difficult to evict them than to tolerate them; their presence at least made the buildings look less abandoned.

The neighborhood, the Jamaica Plain section of Boston, wasn't all that great then. But in the nineteenth century, Germans had flocked there and built breweries, drawn by the promise of pristine water from an underground aquifer called the Stonybrook. Today, Jamaica Plain is a hip and desirable place to live. During the 1980s, it wasn't particularly safe; this was in the middle of the crack epidemic, and half a dozen murders took place within a mile of the brewery our first year.

I had a warehouse, but with only $250,000 to work with, I knew I wouldn't be able to build my own brewery. My dad came up with a great solution: "Jim," he said, "there are plenty of good breweries out there with excellent quality control that aren't working to their full capacity. Why don't you rent time in one of them and brew your beer there? That will give you a foothold until you have the capital to build a brewery of your own." Companies in other food and beverage industries, especially start-ups, contracted out their production lines all the time; the practice was called "co-packing," and it enabled small purveyors just starting out to produce quality products affordably. Contract brewing would make my start-up leaner, and it would also be better for the beer, since a quality established brewery would have a much better brewhouse, cellars, and laboratory that I could use. In addition, our recipe is complex, and my father and I knew we needed a traditional brewery with modern quality control to maintain consistency from brew to brew.

Of the $250,000 I needed, I had $100,000 of my own to invest; I figured I would get a bank loan for the remainder. I stopped in at Cambridge Trust Company, where I had kept a checking account for the better part of twenty years. The loan officer promptly rejected me.

"You don't have collateral, and we don't loan against ideas. We loan against hard assets that we can repossess if you fail."

At least he hadn't said, "*when* you fail."

Okay, I thought, *I'll try somewhere else.* Through a BCG contact, I arranged a meeting with Arthur F. F. Snyder, a vice president at U.S. Trust Company. Art was your classic, crusty old Yankee banker right down to the suspenders. He was rock solid, honest, and fond of sitting back, hooking his thumbs around those suspenders, and proclaiming, "I lend money on the four Cs: character, concept, collateral, and cash." He had been a successful banker for some of the high-tech companies popping up along Boston's Route 128 belt and was known as a man willing to take some risk.

I sat down in Art's wood-paneled office and spent a few minutes telling him about my business plan. Before I could get very far, he stopped me and said, "Jim, I have some bad news. You can go to as many banks as you want, but *nobody* is going to lend you any money."

That was a smack right between the eyes. I politely inquired why.

He sat back in his chair. "Because we're a bank, and we don't get paid to take risks. We get paid to make a profit, and here's how that works. Let's say I lend you $100,000 at 10 percent, I've got to give my depositors 6 percent. It will cost me $2,000 to process the paperwork and administer the loan. So I've got $2,000 profit if nobody defaults. If one loan in fifty defaults, there goes my profit. The only people out there who will lend you money are idiots, and if you want to have a banking relationship with idiots, then good luck!" It was a two-minute explanation of why in those days banks only lent money to solid, safe, ongoing businesses with solid, safe collateral.

With banks out of the picture, I went to see whether a friend of mine at a venture capital firm would help. He looked at the business plan and proclaimed he wasn't interested. When I asked why, he said, "Well, we need to invest in businesses that have at least a reasonable possibility of returning ten times what we put in it. We make ten investments a year, knowing we'll lose our shirts on five of them. Four of them might break even or make double our money. We need *one* that will allow us to make a healthy return—say, ten times our money. And you're not projecting anywhere near a ten-to-one return." From his point of view, my business was all risk and no upside. (I'm not one to gloat, but if he had invested the $100,000 I was looking for that day, his stake as of 2015 would be worth about $400 million.)

I needed to find people who didn't focus on the risks and who could visualize a *little* bit of upside in what I was proposing; I needed investors who cared about Art Snyder's first two Cs—character and concept—over cash and collateral. I wound up getting all the capital I needed from friends and family. Several of my friends within BCG— all junior- or mid-level employees—chipped in seed money, especially after I brought in some trial runs of my beer to taste. A couple of previous BCG employees had started successful companies, so perhaps that made my friends willing to take a risk. Also, I wasn't asking for a lot of money; I took investments as small as $1,000. My friends and family, including my father, each wound up putting in anywhere from $1,000 to $50,000 and receiving limited (non-controlling) partnerships. Those $1,000 investments are now worth about $4 million for the investors who have held on for thirty years.

7

LOOK HARD FOR TALENT.
THEN LOOK AGAIN

ENTREPRENEURS PLANNING NEW BUSINESSES must often decide whether to take on a partner and, if so, whom. I had known from the outset I wanted a partner, since my father had always told me how good it was to have someone with whom to share the highs and lows. I also felt that a partner could contribute some of the skills I didn't have and perhaps have a personality that complemented mine.

So whom should I choose? There was certainly plenty of talent all around me at BCG, the best and the brightest graduates of top business schools. Amazing people went through BCG in these years, political leaders like Mitt Romney and Benjamin Netanyahu, business thinkers like Clay Christensen and George Stalk, and investors like John Paulson. The trouble was that everyone looked more or less like me: good college, good business school (I eventually went back and finished graduate school), a few years of highly paid consulting work. None of them had any experience in the beer industry or even in restaurants or bars—something I would definitely need if my new company was to succeed. Then it hit me: The resumés accumulating on my assistant Rhonda's desk weren't the solution. Rhonda was the solution!

Rhonda Kallman's presence at BCG was a great testament to the way BCG cherished talent. Serving as admin assistant to not one, not two, but seven people, she was smart as a whip, a fast learner, and a good listener. She didn't have a bachelor's degree, but that didn't matter; I had plenty of degrees. Rhonda had something I did not, something they don't teach at Harvard Business School: Rhonda liked bars and she liked people. She was a very determined person—"force of nature" comes to mind. She understood people and what motivated them. She understood bartenders and servers. Plus, she was single and in her early twenties. Bars were her natural habitat.

Many people underestimated Rhonda because she was working as a "secretary" and she liked to party. Yet you underestimated Rhonda at your peril. Confident and self-possessed, she knew how to handle the hyper-achieving, high-anxiety, Type-A business consultants at BCG. With her sharp sense of humor, she had a knack for making people feel comfortable so that they did what she needed them to do, often without even realizing it.

When the idea of bringing Rhonda on as my partner hit me, it struck me as blindingly obvious. Her skills aside, I knew it would be fun to go to battle with her on my team. I first broached the notion of a partnership to her during the spring of 1984, just before I incorporated the company. I had not yet worked out many of the specifics of our operations, so I suppose my offer came across to her as vague or overly idealistic or stupid. She didn't definitively say no, but she made it clear that she was not interested; she valued the stability of her job with BCG and the fun of bartending on the side. She also had serious doubts about whether my idea of a richer, full-bodied, craft-brewed beer would fly. "Jim," she said, "nobody drinks your kind of beer. They drink light beer. There's no room for little guys in the beer industry. I doubt we'd even serve it in the bar where I work."

By the fall of 1984, I had managed to turn Rhonda's tentative "no" into a strong "maybe." Rhonda was back at work after having taken the summer off to hang out and have fun away from the stressful environment of BCG. We were sitting in a bar in Boston's Faneuil Hall neighborhood, and I made the pitch again. She told me her reservations, and I again tried to put them to rest. "Rhonda," I said, "I've never failed at anything in my life, at least not at anything that has been really important to me. I'm not going to fail at this." That show of determination made an impression on her. We agreed that we would firm things up as further details of the business fell into place. But I knew that Rhonda was on board.

We like to think of America as a pure meritocracy, a place where the best talent always wins out. Yet in many cases, the best candidate doesn't get hired; the candidate with the best *education* or the best resumé does. Many companies, beholden to what is essentially an education-based caste system, would never consider Rhonda, who had an associate's degree in secretarial science, for the same job as a Stanford M.B.A. That's a shame. We owe much of Boston Beer's success over the years to Rhonda's energy, drive, and general smarts. Time and again she proved it. She really was the best candidate.

To pick the very best partner, or the best talent for any position, look through all the resumés. Then, before making your final choice, look again. Talent comes in all kinds of packages.

8

THE BEST MARKETING PLAN EVER

PERSUADING RHONDA TO JOIN Boston Beer was my first sales call and, to this day, probably my most important one. Her value to the business became clear immediately, when we sat down together in a bar to sketch out our initial sales efforts. Rhonda again asked the important question: "Who is going to buy this?" I proposed to her what I'd written in my initial business plan: We only had loose cases (we didn't have money to produce six-packs), so we could only target bars and restaurants, not liquor stores. That ruled out 75 percent of the market—not exactly a brilliant strategic move. Among bars and restaurants, we would target places that sold significant quantities of imported beer and were the best at what they did. It wasn't a question of high-end versus low-end establishments. We wanted to be in a premium place like the Ritz-Carlton, but also in the best neighborhood pubs in Boston and the best dive bars—essentially, all the places that offered Bostonians the most authentic, high-quality drinking experiences.

"Sounds great," Rhonda said. "So what specific bars will we call on?"

I flipped through my notes. "Well, we have to be deliberate about it. We'll only be leasing one truck, so we should make a list of a hundred places to hit at first, clustering them in a few neighborhoods to make routing the truck easier."

Rhonda nodded and sipped her beer, digesting what I was saying. "You know what? Hold on a second." She reached into her purse and came up with a stenographer's notebook. Flipping its pages open, she started squiggling furiously in shorthand.

"What are you doing?"

She kept squiggling and squiggling. A few minutes passed, but I didn't interrupt. Finally, she pushed the notebook over to me. "Okay, there you go."

"What's this?" I couldn't read shorthand.

"Our one hundred bars."

I looked at what she'd written. "Seriously? This is incredible. How did you come up with this list?"

She shrugged. "I just walked through the city in my mind. I started at Faneuil Hall, walked around the North Market, the South Market, then up State Street. I went toward the Back Bay up Newbury Street, down Boylston. And then I started doing cross streets."

It was the best marketing plan I'd ever seen before or have seen since. We had a clear, limited, but ambitious goal: Get our beer into these hundred places.

DID WE HAVE TO do this? Why did it matter that we get to every one of them? Why not 90 percent or 95 percent? Why 100 percent? Strictly speaking, I can't argue that we needed to get Samuel Adams into every bar on that list. But there was something about making a commitment and following it through to the very end. I knew it would just *feel* right when we got there even if we had plenty of good, logical reasons to stop before we had Samuel Adams in all one hundred establishments.

There's a big difference between running twenty-six miles and running a marathon even though the actual difference is only 385 yards.

In the ensuing months, we went door to door calling on bars. We would add and subtract bars and restaurants from the list. A couple of places ended up going out of business before we could call on them. But eventually, we wound up getting Samuel Adams into every surviving bar on that original list. Every single one.

9

FIND YOUR YODA

A START-UP ENTREPRENEUR has to juggle a lot of balls. You're not really a chief executive officer, because there's nobody but yourself to execute. The CEO title takes on a new meaning. You're the chief *everything* officer. In my case, starting a beer company required I handle a dizzying array of tasks. I had to get roughly a dozen permits from federal, state, and local authorities in order to brew—a process that took months. I had to arrange for legal and public relations help, choose a good name for my beer, negotiate a lease, figure out how to pay people, find someone to design a label, and so on. All this put me in a tough spot, since as a first-time entrepreneur I'd never done any of it before. I didn't even know what I didn't know, which meant I was bound to make mistakes. Perhaps the greatest challenge of all was figuring out how to take our nineteenth-century recipe and adapt it to twentieth-century brewing equipment and ingredients.

My previous efforts at home brewing hadn't produced anything memorable except my first wife's dismay. Now that I had the recipe from my father, I got serious and started experimenting in our kitchen. The recipe called for me to boil malt, hops, and other ingredients in a large pot (my first brew kettle) for an hour and a half. As the minutes ticked by, the steam from the cauldron filled the kitchen with so much humidity that the wallpaper peeled off in places. My (then) wife wasn't happy, but I was thrilled: One taste of this beer, even though I hadn't yet perfected the recipe, and I was in love. I thought that if I could taste this beer every day of my life, I'd be a happy man.

In the weeks that followed, I brewed several more batches, tinkering with one element or another. Not every batch was successful. On one occasion, the beer exploded in our basement. When you home brew, the final step is to fill the bottles with fermented but flat beer, prime them with a precise amount of sugars, cap them, and let the carbonation build up as the yeast eats all the sugar. I was making an all-malt beer, so I was using maltose instead of sugar, and I miscalculated how much I needed. In a few days, the bottles started exploding: *Pop! Pop! Pop! Pop!* They sounded like muffled grenades. *Oh, man*, I thought. I went carefully downstairs and saw that only a few of the bottles had exploded. What was I to do with the ones still intact? If some of them had blown up, chances were the rest would. I decided to leave them alone. I waited until they all blew up, and then I cleaned up the sticky mess of broken glass and half-dried-up beer.

This failure didn't discourage me; I felt that my experiments with the recipe were successful for the most part. Sometimes when you home brew, you sample your creation and say, "Damn, this tastes terrible!" Not this time. The beer I was making tasted *amazing*. The flavor was complex but balanced. It was assertive—*demanding* attention—in a good way. You might say that it was like hearing rock music for the first time after you've only had Barry Manilow or Kenny G. I didn't know exactly what the final product would become, but I could tell I was on the right track.

I could also tell that I wouldn't realize the potential of this recipe if I continued working alone in my kitchen. I couldn't control temperatures well enough, so the fermentation process wasn't exactly right. In addition, the physics of a five-gallon container—the pressures on the liquid, the diffusion of heat, the caramelization of the sugars—

were different from those of the larger brewing vessels I would need in order to brew at commercial scale. To build a viable business, I would need to take my experimentation to the next level. And I would need to draw on the knowledge of a professional brewing expert. A lot of start-up stories talk about the lone genius founder toiling away in solitude until he has perfected his product and then emerging to dazzle the world. Those stories don't ring true to me, and they weren't my story. I wanted to make uncompromisingly great beer, and I knew it would be a better beer if I had the help of the best brewmaster in the world. So I set out to find him and get his help.

In late 1984, I met Dr. Joe Owades, a renowned brewmaster who had access to a pilot brewery where I could test my recipe. Up until his death in 2005, Joe was respected as one of the world's greatest brewmasters. He held a Ph.D. in biochemistry and had fifty years of experience working for brewers like Rheingold, Miller, and Anheuser-Busch. During the 1960s, he had invented the original light beer for Rheingold Brewery. Years later, Miller Brewing Company ended up owning a large cache of recipes after a series of mergers. The brewers came upon this recipe and gave it a try. Miller's marketing guys re-positioned, renamed, and reintroduced Joe's recipe as *Miller Lite—Everything you ever wanted in a beer and less*.

Given all that Joe had accomplished, I felt he was the ideal person to help me re-create my unique beer. When starting a business, there is probably one thing in a hundred where you need to be the best in the world. The other ninety-nine things, you can be pretty good at. For that one thing, though, it's vital that you get the *very best person in the world* to mentor you and help you achieve perfection. You know Yoda from *The Empire Strikes Back*? You need a Yoda.

For us, brewing was that one thing, and Joe was the Yoda of beer. But getting him on board wasn't easy. When I first called, he said, "I get kids like you calling me all the time who want to get into beer. And I turn them down. Most of them don't know what they're doing—they have no idea." I told Joe about my family history in beer, and about our recipe. He was interested, but not impressed. Then I discovered that his wife was an entrepreneur who also had an M.B.A. from Harvard. That helped. I guess his wife hadn't told him that Harvard M.B.A.s could be bags of hot air like everyone else, because with enough persistence on my part, he finally agreed to become our consulting brewmaster.

It was under Joe's sharp eye at UC Davis that I brewed batches of one third of a barrel (a barrel equals 331 beers). Unfortunately, the results weren't that great. As I wrote in an update to my investors, the batches we created "were not useful for very much. They were way off from what we were intending to brew—too sweet, not enough hops." But it was my first commercial batch. And we had learned enough to keep scaling up.

Joe and I made a trip to the Pittsburgh Brewing Company, the brewery I had selected to contract brew with us. I had checked out other breweries in the Northeast. I needed a brewery that would brew in relatively small batches; otherwise I'd be stuck with too much beer that would go stale before I could sell it. I also needed a brewery that was willing to work with our nineteenth-century recipe, doing a number of things that it had never done before (like using 100 percent malt, noble hops, and traditional brewing practices like kräusening, dry hopping, and a method known as "decoction mashing").

Although I felt good about my choice of Pittsburgh, the brewing process turned out to be a nail-biting experience. There wasn't much room for error; if we were just a little off on the timing, the beer would be out of spec and the $10,000 worth of fine ingredients we purchased would go down the drain. The decoction mashing was especially tricky. To many, "decoction mash" might sound like an unpleasant form of surgery or maybe a dance you'd do at a heavy metal concert. Let me break it down for you: The first step of brewing is to take barley that has been germinated and dried (called "malt"), grind it up, and put it in a big vessel with warm water to create mash. We do this because the hot water in the mash triggers enzymes in the malt to break the grain's complex starches down into simpler sugars. These sugars then become food for the yeast to work on during fermentation.

To obtain a richer, sweeter, fuller-bodied beer like Americans drank in the nineteenth century, you want more sugars to stay in the beer to provide body rather than getting eaten up by the yeast. The sugar molecules have to be small and simple enough for our taste buds to perceive them as sweet, but large and complex enough that the yeast has trouble digesting them. Then you can add the hops and balance out the sweetness with bitterness.

Creating those sugars of a certain size isn't easy when you're working with a large quantity of liquid. Back in the days when the historical figure Samuel Adams was alive, people didn't understand the underlying chemistry, but they had figured out how to brew full-bodied beer by gently taking the mash through a series of carefully calibrated temperature changes. You couldn't do this at once with all the mash in the tub—you couldn't get enough heat into that quantity of liquid in a timely fashion. So according to our family recipe (which reflected old-time brewing practices), you took aside a portion of the liquid and quickly raised the temperature to 212 degrees. When the main tub's mash got to the correct temperature, you pumped back in the boiling "decoction mash" to raise the tub's temperature to 158 degrees within eight minutes. That precise timing ensured that the complex sugars weren't broken down too far into simpler sugars that the yeast would subsequently consume.

By the mid-1980s, decoction mashing had been largely lost to history. It was time-consuming and required an extra brewhouse vessel, so commercial breweries weren't doing it anymore. The big guys were figuring out ingenious ways to maintain consistency while lightening their beers and increasing profitability. When I contracted with Pittsburgh Brewing, I spent $8,000 of my precious capital for the installation of new pipes to brew using the decoction mash method. The brewery already owned an extra vessel that we could repurpose for our decoction mash—that was one of the reasons I chose to brew there (I also liked that the brewery had previously experimented with an all-malt beer of its own, called Sierra). But the brewery needed different pipes and valves, and I didn't know if the equipment would allow us to complete the decoction process within the allotted eight minutes. We're talking about siphoning off a quarter of the overall mash—ten thousand pounds of porridgelike mix—bringing it to a boil, and then piping it back into the main kettle, which was a copper vessel with the capacity of a medium-sized room. Grain only goes so fast through a pipe. If we didn't get it all done within the eight-minute window, I would have wasted $10,000 worth of ingredients.

That first time, Joe Owades and I, along with a couple other people, stood around counting the seconds and watching the temperature rise. Five minutes. Six minutes. Seven minutes. At seven minutes and forty seconds, the temperature reached 158 degrees. It was a close call. But we'd done it!

Once I tasted samples, I knew decoction mashing was worth the hassle. We arrived at a beer with a rich golden amber color, a dense head, and a striking aroma. The taste started with a firm-bodied malt flavor that was balanced with complex hop bitterness, leaving behind a trace of sweetness. It was a classic nineteenth-century lager that tasted the way I guessed the best American beers would have tasted a hundred years earlier.

To this day, even with the hundreds of craft beers Boston Beer Company has brewed, the beer we would eventually call Samuel Adams Boston Lager remains my favorite. I love watching it come out of the tap. I love the thick, muffled sound of the liquid cascading into the glass. There's this alchemy of physics, chemistry, and mathematics—the dynamics of bubbles and aromas. As I look at the glass, I notice a slight, veil-like haze in the liquid comprised of proteins from the malt. The color is amber, with overtones of golds and reds, almost like looking into a candle flame. The aroma is slightly floral, sometimes a dab of red fruit like cherry or raspberry. That first sip wakes up my palate, leading to a three- or four-second parade of the body and sweetness from the malt, followed by spiciness and nuanced bitterness from the hops—not sweet like white sugar, but like caramel, biscuit, toffee, with just a slight roasted note. And then that noble hop aroma and taste with pine, grapefruit, and softer fruits like orange and tangerine, followed by a lingering bitterness at the end that brewers call the "hop signature" of beer.

I've related on television and radio what I taste when I drink Samuel Adams Boston Lager, and the hosts sometimes think I'm crazy. Going on and on like that about beer? Am I overdramatizing it? Actually, I'm not. Back then, people didn't understand that beer can be a taste experience that rivals good wine and delicious food. When someone has taken care with the brewing of a beer, the liquid deserves to be understood and savored. After so many years and all the beers I've tasted, Samuel Adams Boston Lager just never gets old for me.

Often when I drink a glass of Boston Lager, I think back to all that Joe did to help make the beer what it is. Throughout the first couple of years, he accompanied me on many trips to Pittsburgh Brewing, consulting on installation of new equipment and tasting samples when they were ready. As we worked on refining the production process, having Joe by my side was invaluable. He had complete credibility with Pittsburgh Brewing's management. He knew more about brewing than anybody at the brewery.

I don't know if we would have been successful producing Samuel Adams if it weren't for Joe. Not only was he a perfectionist, he had the brewing chops to deliver perfection. It's hard to express all that Joe brought to Boston Lager, and it's also hard to put a dollar value to it. There's a story about a ship whose boilers were not working right, and nobody knew how to fix them. They found a world-famous expert who came in, banged on a pipe with a hammer, and made the boiler come back to life. "That'll be $10,000," the expert said.

The ship's captain was beside himself. "Ten grand? For banging on a pipe? That's an outrage! Send me a bill that justifies the expense."

So the expert sent a bill. He charged $1 for hitting the pipe, and $9,999 for knowing which pipe to hit.

Joe was like that. He knew which pipe to hit, and in exchange for that kind of knowledge and expertise, I paid him as much as I could muster ($7,500 for his services for *all* of 1984) and gave him 2 percent of the company. He more than earned his keep.

10

SACRED COD BOSTON LAGER?

IN EARLY 1985, after I had brewed the first commercial bottles and done the first full-scale test brew, but before I had come up with a name for my new beer, I was wondering how I would get people to drink it. How would they even know about it? I couldn't afford to advertise, but I knew that getting the word out somehow would be almost as critical for success as the beer itself. A brewer in New York told me about public relations firms and how they could help get your story out. I hadn't thought much about the impact that might have, since the foundries and paper mills I had consulted for didn't usually seek publicity. I believed the Koch family heritage and recipe as well as my own determination to upend the beer industry might make for a good story, one that the media might notice if we had a skilled hand on deck dangling newsworthy items before their eyes. I interviewed a couple PR firms and chose Sally Jackson, a respected media relations professional in Boston with many clients in the restaurant and hotel business.

Sally got to work right away, making a list of places where she could open the door and sending out dozens of letters on my behalf. We also worked on coming up with a name. One obvious option was

"Louis Koch Lager," after my ancestor who had created the recipe we were using, but I had already written that one off. People found it difficult to pronounce "Koch." Koch is pronounced like "cook," but some people unthinkingly turn it into an obscenity, so I didn't think "Louis Koch Lager" was such a great name for a product you expect people to put in their mouth—particularly in a long-neck bottle.

Over the previous year, I had been compiling a big list of names, a couple hundred in total, including the one that most people liked, "New World Lager." *New World* was the name of one of the first clipper ships built in Boston and constructed at the Donald McKay shipyard. I had a label designed that featured a ship's bow cutting through the frame of the image, and I also had "New World Lager" business cards printed up to see how it would look. I wasn't sure about the name, and I didn't know anyone with marketing expertise. One of my investors had suggested that I bring in an ad agency to help me. "Jim," he asked me, "are you aware that there are professionals who come up with names for new products? Ad agencies do that all the time."

"Oh, really?" It had never occurred to me that some people could spend all their time just coming up with the right name for a new company or product. Again, not something a foundry needs. I asked Sally, and she directed me to a Boston boutique ad agency called Gearon Hoffman Goransson, whose partners were all ex-bartenders. I told the principals that I wanted a memorable name, one that was assertively American—not some fake European name—and one that would be a strong call at a bar.

They turned their creative talents loose. A couple of weeks later they scheduled a meeting in their conference room where they presented their ideas. This was well before the show *Mad Men*; I had no idea that I'd be treated to a formal presentation, complete with mock-up boards. I sat down while the agency partners stood before me with a buzz of excitement in their eyes.

"Okay," Dan Gearon said, "so we set to work on it, and we went down different paths. We came up with a large group of names, and almost all of them were duds. But we did find the perfect name for your beer, Jim. It's a strong beer call, it's memorable, and it's rooted in Boston's history like no other name. Are you ready to hear it?"

I couldn't wait for this perfect name.

He pulled out a board. His voice deepened with suspense. "The name for your beer, Jim, is . . ." I could almost hear the drum roll. "Sacred Cod!"

"Sacred Cod?" I asked. "Really? Sacred Cod?"

What?! I couldn't believe it. Did they just say *Sacred Cod?* They explained that the Sacred Cod is a state symbol of Massachusetts—a carved wooden codfish that to this day hangs in the Massachusetts State House. Sure, it has history. But a beer named Sacred Cod? Yuck! Who wants to think of stinky fish when they're tossing back a cold one? Even Louis Koch Lager was a better name, and I doubt my great-great-grandfather needed an ad agency to name his beer. Years later, the agency said Sacred Cod was a joke, but they seemed pretty serious at the time.

The three of them offered up several other names that they also thought might work: "Joy Street," "Golden Oak," "Liberty Tree," and the always humorous "Whipping Post." Now *that's* a bar call—"Hey, I need a Whipping Post!"

I went away and pondered all these names. Aside from Sacred Cod, none was terrible, but again, none was an obvious winner to me. I found myself returning again and again to another name on my original list: Samuel Adams. I had long respected the historical figure Samuel Adams for the pivotal role he played in the revolution, all the more so because he was a firebrand and a rabble-rouser whom historians had largely overlooked. Our second president, John Adams, gets the lion's share of the attention given to that family, alongside John's son John Quincy.

My high school history teacher, Miss Graham, a stern Ohio farm lady type with steel-rimmed glasses and long gray hair, used to pass up the more famous American revolutionaries and instead talk about Samuel Adams and Boston. As she reminded us, the Declaration of Independence might have been signed in Philadelphia in 1776, but the "shot heard around the world" occurred in Concord, Massachusetts, in 1775. Thanks in large part to Samuel Adams, Boston had been at war with England for a year before the rest of the colonies caught up. Samuel Adams had been among the first of the Founding Fathers committed to the idea of American independence; he was the propagandist and organizer who stirred up the citizens of Boston to resist the British occupation of the city. After the revolution, he played a major role in the new government, succeeding John Hancock as the governor of Massachusetts. Yet he retained his strong belief in the common people, not the wealthy and well-born, telling his fellow citizens as a newly elected governor, "The sovereignty of a nation, always of right, resides in the body of the People," and "An enlightened, free and virtuous people, can as a body, be the keepers of their own Liberties, and the guardians of their own rights."

I did a little research on Samuel Adams at the Boston Public Library, and the story got even better. Not only had he gone to Harvard, like me, but he had also been involved with making beer. Some books described him as a maltster and others as a brewer. To me, this was fate: a brewer and a revolutionary. Samuel Adams became my top choice.

At the same time, I still liked New World Lager and was open to considering a few of the ad agency's options. Since people around me offered conflicting opinions, I resolved to do some primitive market research by taking my names from bar to bar. I'm a big believer that if you have an important decision to make, you should find a way to validate your instincts. A woman who worked at BCG, Gail Hutchinson, was a graphic artist who had offered to mock up a label for New World and now for Samuel Adams. The result was the basic structure of the present-day label, complete with a rough likeness of Samuel Adams as its centerpiece. She charged me $400.

Depicting Samuel Adams was a problem for me initially; I couldn't find a suitable likeness of the man. I had found a portrait of Adams dating from his years as a governor, but none from his younger days as a brewer and rabble-rouser. The closest thing was the statue of Samuel Adams that stands in front of Boston's Faneuil Hall. I took some photos of the statue and gave them to an illustrator in New York City that the ad agency recommended. I also sent him a book of portraits by John Singleton Copley and asked him to do the portrait in that style. He came back with the image of Samuel Adams in his brewers' vest, a version of which still appears on every bottle of Samuel Adams Boston Lager.

Meanwhile, the agency mocked up handmade labels for several other names. In February 1985, we pasted all the labels onto bottles and I went around to bars asking customers, bartenders, managers, and waitstaff for their opinions. The verdict wasn't clear—some people liked Samuel Adams, some New World Lager, and some the other names on our list. I'll also never forget one guy who looked at our Samuel Adams label and said, "It's never gonna sell. 'Cause *guys* drink beer. You need to put a phallic symbol on there. You need the Bunker Hill Monument. Call it Bunker Hill Beer; put that big, tall, straight monument right there on the label."

Walking around with a six-pack of beers with different labels and names may not sound like high-quality consumer research, but it's actually better than most of what you find in professional research reports—all those graphs, charts, and complicated verbiage that companies pay big bucks for. I had personally talked to almost two hundred people over five nights of barhopping. I had heard the tone of their voices and picked up on their body language. When I added up the numbers, New World and Samuel Adams had roughly equal numbers of votes. But I sensed those who liked Samuel Adams felt more passionately about their choice.

I headed home one weekend knowing I had to decide. All entrepreneurs experience moments like this: times when outside experts, as valuable as they are, can't help you; times when you have to look inward and go with what *feels* right. Most of the really important business decisions come down to judgment. Your brain is no smarter than your gut—you need both. And I had educated my gut by talking to two hundred real human beings.

I chose Samuel Adams, concluding that it was stronger and more deeply rooted in history than New World Lager. The New World label was prettier, but Samuel Adams Boston Lager suggested that I wanted to "throw the foreign beers out," just as our Founding Fathers wanted to throw the Brits out. Plus, it felt *better* to go into a bar and ask for a Samuel Adams. It was as simple as that. I said that Samuel Adams Boston Lager may or may not have been a drop-dead name, but it was a good name, and a year from then we would think of it as the drop-dead name. I look back at that decision now, and Samuel Adams does feel completely right.

I wonder where we would be today if we had gone with Sacred Cod.

11

THE DIFFERENCE BETWEEN SEX AND MASTURBATION

IN BUSINESS SCHOOL, people tend to talk about business in the abstract. They talk about "markets" and "demand" and "consumer sectors" and "demographics." Yet I believed something else: Markets and their associated concepts don't exist. Let me repeat that: *Markets don't exist!* What *do* exist are flesh-and-blood customers. I could talk about markets all I wanted, but I could only sell beer to bartenders and bar managers. You can't sell to a market, only to a person, because markets don't buy beer. People buy beer.

Likewise, marketing doesn't sell products. Selling coupled with the delivery of *real value* sells products. I was guest lecturing a class at Harvard Business School once when a slightly smug and annoying student complimented me on my "great marketing." It's a backhanded compliment people have often paid me over the years, and I always find it misguided because it implies that the marketing is more important than the beer. This is not true; *the beer* is what has made us successful. In fact, we didn't hire our first marketing person until 1994—ten years after we started. There's an old saying: "Nothing kills a bad product faster than good marketing." We've done good advertising and bad advertising, good marketing and bad marketing. But the beer has always been good, and our sales force is the best in the business.

Anyhow, this student was waiting for a response, so I took a breath and calmly gave him my standard response about the quality of the beer and the importance of sales over marketing. This theory fell on deaf ears. The student countered that good marketing was critical and sales was, well, a "low function task." And then he told me that sales was just an extension of marketing. "What's the difference between marketing and sales?" he challenged.

My blood boiled. I thought for a minute, and a metaphor popped into my head that I thought was perfect (inappropriate, but perfect). I've since repeated it often—to the horror of more than a few unsuspecting audiences, including (what was I thinking?) two hundred people who had gathered at the Library of Congress (and had probably paid good money) to hear me speak.

I looked at this student and said, "I'll tell you the difference. The difference between marketing and sales is the difference between masturbation and sex." I think I heard a couple of gasps. Good! I wanted people's attention. So I kept going: "One you can do all by yourself in a dark room and fool yourself into thinking you're accomplishing something. The other requires real human skills and all the fury and muck and mire of real human-to-human contact."

Entrepreneurs need to focus on what's real. You shouldn't worry so much about the image or hype that exists *around* the product or service. You should focus on the product, and on selling it. A great sales force can't sell without a great product—it's like a race car running off crappy gasoline. Great salespeople are only effective when they know they're selling something worth buying.

To this day, one of the mantras at the Boston Beer Company is: "The main thing is to keep the main thing the main thing." And that main thing was and *is* brewing and selling a quality beer. A *"Wow!"* product will beat *"Wow!"* marketing. Always.

PART II

BOILING AND COOLING

(1985-1988)

Once you have created a sweet mash, you separate the liquid from the grain and leave the grain behind. This liquid, the "wort," is then pumped to the brew kettle, where it is mixed with hops and brought to a boil to bring together the ingredients. You send it through a whirlpool to remove the spent hops and coagulated proteins from the malt. Then you cool it. The cooling is vital, because if the liquid is too hot, yeast will die. Like a company in the process of starting up, wort is simple potential. The flavors of the finished beer have not yet formed, and you have no idea whether what you're making will be worth drinking. But you can't wait to find out.

STRING THEORY

THERE'S A STORY I like involving the writer Kurt Vonnegut. Maybe it's true, maybe not, but it's a good story. So I'll tell it. He was at a party, seated next to a very rich guy who was bragging nonstop about his wealth and possessions. He had bought a Picasso, he said, to hang in his guest bathroom. Vonnegut finally interrupted, "You know, I have something you would really love to have, but I don't think you're ever going to be able to have it."

"What do you have?" the guy asked. He was ready to shell out the dough to buy anything Vonnegut had, just so he could say he had one, too.

"I have *enough.*"

How right Vonnegut was. One of the first life lessons I learned as an Outward Bound instructor is that material possessions are highly overrated. You can live a good, full life owning nothing more than you can fit into your car. Simple as that. A lot of the stuff we think we need *gets in the way* of happiness. Excessive consumption tends to distract us from what's really important: building a life and helping others. Consumption can also lead to vanity and pride, insulating us from people who have less than we do. I know, for instance, that I was completely happy staying in a fifty-dollar-a-month rooming house during the 1970s because I had freedom to work on things that mattered to me, and I was motivated to try to master them.

On the trail, I learned something else: Even basic survival doesn't require nearly as many possessions as we usually think. Let me describe a principle I call my "String Theory." We emphasized self-reliance at Outward Bound, so we didn't carry the latest and greatest equipment. The equipment was solid and functional, but there was nothing fancy. Among other things, we got a supply of string called "alpine cord." This string served many purposes, including letting you hang a tarp, support a tent, string up food at night, lash items to a backpack, and fix items that may have broken. As instructor, I was in charge of handing out the string and other supplies. Before long, I noticed something important. If, at the outset, I gave the patrol plenty of string, it would run out before the end of the twenty-eight-day course. As an experiment, I decided to try it the other way around. I gave a patrol less string than they would need, and I told them the supply was short. What happened? They finished the trip with string to spare.

How was this? Well, the members of my group with a surplus of string had wasted it. Maybe they cut it carelessly, leaving themselves with odds and ends that were too small to be usable. Maybe they didn't keep an eye on their string and left portions of it behind on a tree. Maybe they never learned to use this scarce resource efficiently. The waste became a habit and part of the group culture. On the other hand, when I didn't pass out enough string, people in my group used it much more carefully. They even picked up pieces of string left behind by earlier groups and tied them together. They devised new solutions to minimize their use of string, and best of all, they shared string with others so that no one had too much or too little.

This taught me that culture and values can substitute for money and resources. And a small company with great culture and values can beat much bigger companies that are flush with money and resources. It's the strength of the weak.

That's my String Theory, and it's especially important to keep in mind as an entrepreneur.

When I started Boston Beer, I had to make my seed money last. That meant Rhonda and I would have no other employees helping us—we wore lots of hats. We didn't spend money renting office space, because we didn't need it. Rhonda and I were out making sales calls every day and hosting "Meet the Brewer" nights in bars most evenings (as I once said, "I can't sell beer to a desk"). Or I was in Pittsburgh at the brewery. Cellular telephones were just beginning to appear, and both Rhonda and I had phones installed in our cars, in addition to relying on pay phones between sales calls and hiring a service to answer a landline. We didn't have an actual office for almost a year.

We certainly didn't buy computers or have a bookkeeping or payroll system; I just wrote a check to Rhonda every week for her gross salary with no taxes or Social Security taken out. I didn't want to waste half a day waiting in line at the Social Security Administration to set up an employer's account, and then go to Workers' Compensation and waste another half-day there, and then waste still more time at another government agency. I figured that if we went belly up, the IRS probably wouldn't care about us—we were too small. If we succeeded, we could hire an accountant to clean up the mess and keep me out of jail. That I worried about any of this revealed just how little I knew about starting a business. Not long after we'd hired our first employee, I was complaining to a bar owner about the bureaucracy of a single employee, and he said, "Jim, you don't have to do any of that stuff. Don't you know there's something called payroll services? They probably charge you just $200 a year for one employee."

"Ohhh," I said, a little sheepishly. There I was, a well-educated management consultant who couldn't figure out how to set up a payroll.

I could have arranged to fund an office and computers. I chose not to, turning down additional money that investors—including my father—offered. I knew that the more money I took from investors, the more ownership I would give up. Something similar occurs on the mountain trail: Any resources you have available to you come with some kind of cost. The string and the other supplies I gave out cost money, and they also added to physical weight we had to carry. More was clutter. It slowed you down and got in the way. Less was more.

As I told Rhonda and my investors, I didn't want us to "play company." Many enterprises, both start-ups and established firms, distract themselves with all the trappings of being in business—like offices, support "systems," and other clutter. I knew from Outward Bound that I was just as likely to succeed—even more likely—if I cut it close to the bone. I constantly asked myself, "Do I really need this?" I focused on only two things: making great beer and working our butts off to sell it. I would spend money on these things without hesitation, but on nothing else. If something didn't help me do what was best for the beer, it wasn't a priority. End of story.

Adhering to a strict financial and strategic discipline isn't easy. Sometimes we lapse, and when we do, it's often on account of an emotion like fear. In early March 1985, just as I was getting ready to close up my office at BCG for good, Rhonda and I received an initial shipment of beer from Pittsburgh—forty-eight cases—to use as samples. Our finished labels weren't yet ready, so the bottles came with generic white labels marked "SAMUEL ADAMS SAMPLE BREW" in thick black print. It was thrilling finally to taste the beer and hold a bottle of Samuel Adams in my hand, but it was also scary. We had 1,260 cases out of our initial brew of 4,000 scheduled to arrive a few weeks later, in time for Patriots' Day (a holiday in Massachusetts), and they weren't going to grow legs and walk out of our warehouse on their own. Someone would need to sell them one case at a time, one bar at a time. And that someone couldn't just be Rhonda; it would also have to be me.

Overeducated people at the time thumbed their noses at sales-people, seeing them as manipulative, unscrupulous, and dishonest hucksters. The dominant image of a salesman was Willy Loman from the play *Death of a Salesman*. What little kid wanted to be Willy Loman when he grew up? I knew what my business-school classmates would think when they heard I'd given up a promising career to peddle beer bar to bar. Harvard Business School offered many classes on marketing but not a *single* course on selling. That remains true today, an indication that the cultural image of the salesman hasn't improved all that much over the years. Just think of some of the movies: *The Wolf of Wall Street*, *American Hustle*, and *Glengarry Glen Ross*. I loved the idea of brewing, but selling? No.

My trepidation didn't just relate to status but to my near-total lack of experience in sales. As a kid with a lawn business, I had gone house to house in search of customers, but they had been neighbors, not strangers. I hadn't sold anything as an adult, and I didn't have the fog-giest idea what it meant to sell beer to bars. I was a consultant living in a leafy Boston suburb with two small children; I didn't hang out in bars at night. How would I connect with a bartender? And how would I sell what was then a pretty strange new product? In 1984, starting a beer company was an outrageous idea, like starting a car company. When I called on bars, I would have to reinvent for them the whole concept of what a beer company was. I imagined many people wouldn't get it, and I would have bartenders and managers slamming the door in my face. I wasn't so sure I was up for that.

I initially thought I might be able to avoid the pain of rejection by signing up a distributor to sell my beer for me. That was a nonstarter. Since so few small breweries existed back then, distributors weren't jumping at the chance to spend their precious time and energy selling my unknown beer. Not a single one of the five distributors in Boston would work with me. It didn't help that my beer looked and tasted unfamiliar to them, that I couldn't afford to print six-packs, and that distributors preferred selling six-packs to liquor stores rather than loose cases to bars and restaurants. Oh, and my beer had a funny name. And a different taste. And was the most expensive beer in the market. Oh, yes, and I had no money for advertising, which is what distributors thought you needed.

As distributor after distributor turned us down, I started feeling discouraged. "Fuck it, Jim," Rhonda finally said. "Why can't we do it ourselves?"

"How?" I asked.

"Can't we just start our own distributorship?"

So that's what we did, which meant I had to lease a truck, buy some handcarts, and start selling. The selling didn't go so well at first. In fact, it didn't happen at all. Just after the samples came in, my uncle Jim Kautz called me up to see how I was doing. Uncle Jim had started with Goldman Sachs back in the '60s, selling fixed-income bonds to entrepreneurs and small businesses, and had risen to become one of the firm's senior partners. He had always been a mentor to me; I respected his deeply ingrained values of integrity and honesty. He was not naturally outgoing, unlike many salespeople, but rather a little reserved in an old-school, German way.

"So, Jim," he said, "what did you do today?"

I told him that I had gone up to New Hampshire (to avoid paying Massachusetts sales tax) to shop for a computer. Yes, I was on the verge of violating my String Theory—that's how fearful I had become.

"Why do you need a computer, Jim?"

"Well, to keep track of sales and receivables."

There was a pause on the line. "Ah, sales. Jim, do you have any sales?"

"No, not yet."

"Well, maybe you should get some first before you buy a computer." I wasn't convinced, but he wouldn't hear any counterarguments. "Jim," he told me, "I've seen a lot of businesses go broke. They all had plenty of computers. They went broke because they didn't have enough sales. Forget about the computer; go get some sales!"

He was right: I had been playing company for weeks, doing anything to avoid making cold calls at bars.

The only way to stop playing company was to confront my fears. Uncle Jim told me that he, too, had felt uncomfortable cold-calling when he first started out. He advised that I set a modest goal for myself: one new customer a day. And don't come home until you get one or the bars close. And if you get one early, you can take the rest of the day off.

I got off the phone and resolved to put that plan into action. But I wouldn't do it that day . . . I would wait until the next day. I needed to prepare. I went to the Harvard Business School bookstore and found the only book they had on sales, Tom Hopkins's *How to Master the Art of Selling*. It had a guy on the cover who looked like the stereotypical salesman: square jawed, smiling, maybe a little manipulative, and wearing a suit that looked like polyester. But it was the only book on selling in the whole Harvard Business School bookstore, so I bought it. It had practical techniques about how to open and close a selling conversation—objection handling, different kinds of closes (like the puppy dog close and the Ben Franklin close), the kinds of things that salespeople usually get trained in. A lot of it seemed a little cheesy to me, but I followed Hopkins's advice and created and memorized a thirty-second sales pitch so I would know exactly what to say when I went in.

"Hi, I'm Jim Koch, and I'm starting a brewery here in Boston to make a new beer called Samuel Adams Boston Lager. Have you heard of it?" The book said to ask questions early in the conversation, and to offer something tangible the customer could pick up and hold. So if the bar manager said he hadn't heard of my beer, I planned to take out a little folder with reprints from our initial press exposure. "Well, we're actually starting to get some publicity in publications your customers might be reading." A bar manager could pick up the article and read it. If he seemed receptive, I'd ask him if he'd like to taste the beer. If he replied with "Send me a bottle and I'll try it,"

I would surprise him. "Even better," I'd say, "I've got a bottle right here." If he said, "Well, leave it here so it can get cold," I'd surprise him *further* by saying, "I have cold packs in my briefcase, so it's cold already."

After he tasted it, I planned to ask him what he thought. I felt confident he'd like it, in which case I'd ask if he thought it was good enough to sell to his customers (the book told me to ask questions that were easy to say "yes" to). If the bar manager said "no", then fine, he didn't like my beer and I wouldn't waste my time trying to convince him. But if he liked it, then I'd close by asking him how many cases he needed. Even one case was a start.

There it was: my big plan. Unfortunately, having a plan didn't make my task any easier. I woke up the next morning with a sense of dread. *Oh, man*, I thought, *I really want to stay in bed!* I got up and went into my office at BCG to procrastinate for a few hours longer (I was winding down my work at BCG on a part-time basis, so I still had my office). Rhonda told me I shouldn't call on a bar or restaurant first thing in the morning, since the staff wouldn't be in early after closing the previous evening well past midnight. Around 11 o'clock, I realized it was time. I had the cold beer in my nice consultant's briefcase. I had plastic cups. I told myself I had to do this.

My soon-to-be-former office at BCG was on the thirty-third floor of a beautiful new building that overlooked the Boston Harbor. I stood up at my desk, dressed in my navy blue consultant's suit, and took in the spectacular view. *All right*, I thought, *I will probably never have an office this nice again for the rest of my life. I'm working for CEOs, I have Jack Welch at General Electric as a client, I make a handsome salary, I fly first class—and as of now, I'm leaving this behind. I am now a beer salesman.*

I did feel a little relieved. I had enjoyed consulting work and felt I was making a difference, but the nice office and first-class airfare and fancy hotels were just distractions, not an end in themselves. Good riddance.

I allowed myself another moment to take in the view before heading for the elevator.

A few minutes later, as I was outside walking down Congress Street in downtown Boston, I thought, *Okay, it's done. Now, I'm one more schmuck selling beer, just in a fancy suit.*

I came to the corner of State Street, looking for a bar. I couldn't see any, so I walked down State, telling myself I was going to walk into the first bar I came to. And there it was: the Dockside. I went inside, finding myself in a long, narrow space with a bar area in front. An old-school bar. No food, no ferns. I said hello to the man behind the bar and introduced myself, getting a strange nod in response. I started talking. It turned out he only spoke Spanish and didn't understand anything I was saying. He was the barback, the rough equivalent of a busboy in a restaurant. I didn't know any better and started my carefully practiced sales call.

The manager was in back watching us; he must have wondered who this guy in the dark suit was and feared that I was from the Internal Revenue Service or Immigration and Naturalization Service. Who else would be chatting up his barback so enthusiastically? He approached me, told me he was the manager, and asked me what I wanted. I started my sales pitch again. "Hi, I'm Jim Koch. I'm starting a beer company here in Boston . . ."

The man glanced at the magazine articles I showed him and agreed to sample my beer. "Leave it here. I'll chill it and drink it later."

"I brought you a cold sample," I said. "And I have some cups." I had learned about the presumptive close, and I really believed that he would say yes if he tasted my beer.

I poured the beer, knowing that if you poured a beer, people would at least taste it.

Guess what? He liked it! "Kid," he said, "I like your story, but I didn't think the beer was going to be this good. I'll take it."

Thank God! If he'd told me it was snake piss and nobody would ever drink it, I might have gone back to BCG and asked for my old job back.

I shook his hand, thanked him very much, and left. I was thrilled. *I had my first customer! It was easy! Amazing.*

I walked back to the office, relieved, and told Rhonda. "Rhonda, guess what? We have our first sale!"

"That's great, Jim. How many cases did you sell?"

Oh, shoot.

I had been so happy that I forgot to ask the manager how many cases he wanted.

Rhonda laughed at my rookie mistake. "Looks like you'll have to go back and find out."

I did go back the next day, scared out of my mind that the bar manager would change his mind. Fortunately for me, he didn't. He ordered five cases. I had done it: my first sale.

I wasn't playing company any longer.

THE STRING THEORY is difficult to maintain as a company grows. Core beliefs and practices get lost or diluted, and success goes to people's heads. You wind up spending money on things you plain don't need. As your start-up takes root, work on keeping your operations as simple as possible. Even today, when people come to me proposing new initiatives or capital investments, I always ask, "Is that a 'nice to have' or a 'need to have'?" Competing against gigantic companies, we don't have the luxury of carrying "nice to haves." Nor can we afford the distraction that comes with excess spending. Extra offices, departments, equipment, personnel: All these eat up resources and prevent people from paying attention to the aspects of our business that really do add value. When was the last time you looked for something at home and had trouble finding it because you had too much other stuff in the way? The same thing happens at companies.

The String Theory has affected the way I look at and manage both business and personal travel. Over the years, my family and I have traveled to faraway places like Africa, China, and Latin America. I travel beyond light. This might seem hard to believe, but if I'm going away on a weeklong trip to several cities, I'll leave with only my nylon briefcase in hand. I never check a bag; I don't even take a carry-on. I just have my briefcase. It will hold five of everything I need to change daily—shirts, socks, etc. No spare pants or blazer. If I spill something, I get the stain out in the hotel. A little sandwich bag contains toiletries, medications, and so on. If I'm going somewhere cold, I take a down jacket and a rain jacket that go into a stuff-sack the size of a grapefruit. Finally, I bring along a spare credit card and driver's license, so I can still finish the trip if I forget or lose my wallet (I've done that).

Having to carry only a briefcase simplifies travel. Everything is with me and in one place, easy to keep track of. In all my years of travel, I've never lost my briefcase. From time to time, I go through it and weed out stuff I no longer need, just as I used to do from my backpack when I got home after a climb. As of this writing, I carry only an iPad with me. It has taken five pounds out of my briefcase, replacing my OAG pocket travel guide, a laptop, an extra battery and charger for the laptop, a financial calculator, and my iPod. I just don't need the stuff. (Thank you, Steve Jobs.)

The Latin word for luggage is *impedimenta*—"impediment." Why would you impede yourself either in business or in life? I say you should pack for business travel—and run a business—the way you would pack for a climb: Take what you need. Travel lighter, travel faster. No "nice to haves" to slow you down.

13

"I MAKE MY MONEY WHEN I BUY THE GOODS"

I'VE LEARNED A LOT from my customers. Perhaps this comes from listening to them first and trying to understand their business before trying to sell them anything. I'm particularly grateful to the owner of Kappy's, a big liquor store in Boston. In the early days of Sam Adams, I went into his store to see if I could persuade the owner that carrying Samuel Adams would be good for his business. I was expecting a tough sell, but he immediately agreed he should have my beer in his store. Then he told me he had one very important request. He noticed that my best deal was on a twenty-five-case order. He asked if I would give him seventy-five cents a case off that price if he ordered fifty cases.

He said, "I'll give you a prime spot, and I'll call in my orders so you won't have to come back every week." I calculated that it cost me about $25 to make a delivery and about $15 to make a sales call. I did the quick math; he would save me forty bucks, and I'd give him back $37.50. I agreed immediately, since I would be making a little more money with him and anyone else who moved up to the larger quantity.

I then asked him why the seventy-five cents a case was so important, especially since he was selling a case for an eight-dollar profit. He smiled, as if he had been waiting for that question. "You don't understand my business. I have the best prices and expensive rent, but I still make more money than my competition. Young man, I don't make my money when I *sell* the goods, I make my profit when I *buy* the goods. That seventy-five cents is my profit."

I had never thought about business that way, but he was right. I had been so focused on making and selling my beer, I hadn't thought about the rest of the equation. At that point, I was making something like 10 percent profit on my sales. Sixty-five percent of revenue went into the cost of the packaged beer, and my other costs were about 25 percent, so there was 10 percent left.

I decided to look at every place we spent money. I found money everywhere! It was like opening all the drawers in your house and finding a pile of cash in every one. Occasionally, it was as simple as asking for a lower price. Usually, it required that I be a better customer. For example, I had sixty-day terms with our contract brewery because I needed the extra time to pay, but once we were profitable, I asked for and got a 5 percent lower price by paying in five days. I found a way to use lighter-weight bottles of equal strength, and that saved 15 percent on bottles. We got our wholesalers to contribute twenty-five cents a case to help support the salespeople we put in their market. The list went on and on, and a year later we were making twenty cents on every dollar of sales. By learning to make money when we bought the goods, we doubled our profit.

14

THE STRENGTH OF THE WEAK

RHONDA AND I PRESOLD a surprising amount of beer those few weeks before our first big shipment arrived. Of course, most of the bar managers and owners either wouldn't see me or just said no. But some believed, as we did, that a segment of drinkers out there would want more flavorful beer if only they knew it existed. Unless people had traveled abroad, they had never experienced a beer like this. The bars were also attracted to the idea of buying beer from a start-up company; they liked giving the underdog a chance to succeed and enjoyed the personal touch of being called on by the president of the company. "I don't think you're going to make it," some of them said, "but August Busch and Pete Coors have never been in my bar, so I'll give you a shot." Others asked me if I made Samuel Adams in my bathtub. And some offered to take my beer to "help me out."

I figured Rhonda and I could service up to thirty accounts initially, and I hoped to have lined up twenty bars or restaurants by the time the first big shipment of beer came. By late March 1985, we had landed those twenty, and by April 10, when the beer finally arrived, we had thirty. I had anticipated selling two or three cases per account per week initially, and we were doing more than that—almost five.

I knew sales would fall off from that initial order, that it would prob-ably settle down to four cases per account per week, since some drink-ers would try Samuel Adams and then go back to what they had been drinking. But given that the initial number of accounts was higher than forecast, Boston Beer Company's total sales would start slightly ahead of what I'd hoped.

On April 10, when the truck drove up and the driver flung open the back door, I caught my first glimpse of all those cases of beer, stacked into their pallets, with the real Samuel Adams labels on them. After eighteen months of hard work, it was an incredible sight. And a daunting one. I had been making inroads in sales, but the orders I was taking were mostly for three to five cases. At that rate, it would take two or three months to sell all this. I pushed that thought from my mind because there was a more immediate problem. Someone had to move the pallets from the truck, through a building, and then through a narrow doorway into our windowless first-floor warehouse.

If you dream of becoming an entrepreneur, be prepared to handle a lot of things you've never done before and probably don't have a clue how to do. To move those pallets, I rented a forklift and taught myself how to drive it—more or less. I had grown up driving tractors, but a forklift is a different animal; a forklift steers using its rear wheels and the load in front blocks your view. The doorway was seriously narrow. I took half a dozen bricks out of the doorway when I misjudged the position of the left fork. I looked at that jagged doorway for years as a reminder of my own incompetence. Yet once I got the hang of it, I began to enjoy scooting around the warehouse stacking beer. It was like the first time my grandfather let me drive the tractor on his farm.

The improvisation did not end there, and it didn't only involve me. During the first few months, Rhonda and I fell into a division of labor to get the beer sold and shipped to customers. Both of us helped on the delivery truck, and we sometimes made sales calls jointly. She would open up the conversation, and I would pick it up from there. After the call, we'd debrief one another, talking about what had worked and what hadn't. This way, we taught ourselves, little by little, how to sell.

Selling our beer turned out to require far more time and energy than was the norm in the beer business. The big breweries generated consumer demand through advertising—what marketing professors call a "pull" strategy, as opposed to "pushing" the product directly through sales. Although breweries had sales forces, their people didn't spend much time in the field. Mostly they sat in their offices, evaluating the sales numbers, making reports, tracking budgets, maintaining inventories, and making sure orders got shipped—in other words, playing company. Even today, I rarely see anyone from the big breweries actually selling beer. The advertising is supposed to do that.

Lacking any money for advertising, Rhonda and I focused on building deep and personal relationships with our accounts, educating them about our beer and helping our customers build interest in our beer on the grassroots level. Once a bar agreed to serve our beer, we spent hours in the place ourselves, meeting with drinkers and holding blind taste tests in which we put our beer up against the leading imports. We almost never lost, and people were amazed to find that our beer really was higher quality. Education, we realized, was critical. I had to explain to both drinkers and bartenders and managers (who recommended products to drinkers) what made our beer so special. We didn't just need to get people to drink our beer; the sale wasn't really complete until the bottle was empty.

As part of our presentation, I brought in hops and malt and let drinkers touch and taste them for themselves (you can still do this today if you visit our Boston brewery). On other occasions, Rhonda and I would conduct training sessions with bartenders, waitstaff, and others, inviting them to taste our beer and teaching them about our brewing process and our special ingredients. Some of these sessions took place in three minutes during a shift change, while others lasted as long as thirty minutes. It was the sort of tactic some vineyards were using to sell wine during the 1980s, but nobody had yet thought to do

it for beer. As I would tell bar managers and owners, "Your staff probably has never sold a beer like this. You obviously want them to sell a
lot, since it's your highest-priced and most profitable beer. Let me help
educate your staff and make them comfortable selling it to drinkers."
Staff members liked the training; since our beer was the most expensive and better tasting, they got higher check totals and bigger tips by
selling more of it.

As we did more of these presentations, Rhonda and I got to the
point where we could finish one another's sentences. Rhonda sometimes talked about the technical side of brewing: decoction mash,
kräusening, dry hopping. After she mentioned dry hopping, you'd
always hear a little snicker. And if I mentioned dry hopping and there
was a snicker, Rhonda would light a smile and say, "And that's not
what we used to have to do in high school!"

We also helped bars sell our beer by giving customers grassroots
promotional materials like T-shirts, painters' hats, and bottle openers.
Every bottle we sold came with a small hangtag that informed drinkers about the beer they were drinking. We couldn't afford the costs of
artwork and printing, so we hand-made posters for display in bars,
taking uncut sheets of labels, gluing a block of them onto a foam
board, and affixing the bar's name in rub-off Letraset letters (this was
before color printers and desktop publishing). Rhonda and I would make
these posters ourselves at my house on Saturdays, and my two kids,
who were small then, would climb all over them and sometimes help us.

An even more important tool—and one we sort of fell into using—
was the table tent. Table tents are the little paper A-frame-shaped
things you sometimes see in bars and restaurants. I had noticed almost immediately that if I put up table tents in a bar, I usually got a
five-case order the next week. If I didn't, I received only a three-case
order. Table tents increased our sales by 66 percent! We made table
tents a standard part of our ground game. Since we could only afford
to print black-and-white, I designed table tents with text that explained
our ingredients and brewing process. That way, people could learn

about our beer while waiting for the server to take their order. A printer in South Boston made the table tents cheaply for us, using a century-old press that had been idle for years. Because the type was set by hand, we could customize them for each account, something no other brewer had ever bothered to do. At one point, my trunk had more than fifty boxes of table tents, each for a single bar. Each said something like, "The Union Oyster House proudly serves America's only classic lager, Samuel Adams Boston Lager."

The same thing happened when we started selling in stores. As a small-volume brand, we were typically placed on the very top or very bottom shelf. I noticed that if I asked the manager if I could rearrange the shelf and move our beer to eye level, our sales quadrupled! Wow! I knew there was no amount of advertising—even a three-million-dollar Super Bowl ad—that could have that kind of impact on sales.

Hitting drinkers at the moment of truth, when they were choosing a beer, leveled the playing field a bit with our larger competitors. To my way of thinking, it was *way* more effective than advertising and marketing. The general principle—and something we continue to practice to this day—was to make sure we were as visible as possible in the places where people went to buy and drink their beer. In a bar, that might mean table tents. In a store it might mean working hard to get shelf space at eye level. Pretty obvious, I know, but as I like to say, sometimes the obvious answer *is* the obvious answer. Make Sam Adams available and visible. When you try to complicate it, you mess up.

Without knowing it, we were improvising a new way of generating demand, as innovative in the industry as our beer itself was. It was an end run around the big brewers, an approach I came to call "the strength of the weak." Forget about the enormous ad budgets and huge sponsorship deals, the babes in bikinis and sophomoric humor. We were doing something the big guys couldn't do. We could care about every account. They could carpet bomb the market with their big ad budgets, but we could win the hand-to-hand combat, the ground war. It was person-to-person selling and execution based on education and product quality. And it was an approach so potent that today's small craft brewers continue to employ it. We could carve out a niche for ourselves against the odds, but it would mean grinding it out, winning over one bar at a time. Every bar, in effect, was a test. We either passed or failed. And we were determined to pass.

Thirty years later, we still are.

15

THE GOLDEN RULE
OF SELLING

AS A CONSULTANT, I had created business strategies for large companies facing tough problems they couldn't figure out on their own. Pretty heady stuff, but nothing compared to walking into a bar, interacting with bar managers, changing attitudes, and convincing them to embrace our beer. Within thirty seconds, I had to figure out the role of the person I was talking to, what kind of influence he or she had on the decision-making process, what the bar was all about, who the clientele was, and how the bar made money. And once I had figured out these things, the next step was to determine how Samuel Adams Boston Lager could help them accomplish their objectives.

Some people see sales as morally dubious because they think it's about merely pushing a product. Not true. Done right, selling is about helping customers. I believed that Boston Beer Company would make the most money possible over the long term if we gave bar managers a product that genuinely helped them accomplish *their* objectives, and if we followed through to make sure those objectives were met. This is the Golden Rule of Selling: Never ask customers to do something that is not in their long-term best interest. Businesses should adhere to an almost Buddhist ideal of selflessness. If you do that, as we did from the outset, you make life a lot easier for yourself. You build trusting, loyal relationships with people. You wind up winning financially because your customers benefit from the relationship. And perhaps most importantly, you feel good about selling because you are helping others succeed as well.

To help your customers accomplish their objectives, take time to listen carefully and understand what customers perceive their needs to be. Remember, people do what they do for their own good and sufficient reasons, and not everybody benefits from buying what you're selling. Until you understand people's reasons for doing what they're doing, you have no ability to change their beliefs and behavior. You're just arguing, and you're not going to win. People will hang on to their beliefs until they're given a good reason not to. If a prospective customer won't benefit from your product or service, stop selling, say thank you, and move on.

Creating the right sales relationships wasn't easy for us. It entailed two basic tasks. First, we needed to make sure we were right for a particular bar. Rhonda and I decided we didn't want to be in all two thousand bars and restaurants in Boston, but in a much smaller number of high-quality, authentic places that represented a good match for our product. As we made our way through our initial list of prospects, and as we expanded into new neighborhoods and added other bars to the list, we had to learn how to discriminate among establishments, even if it meant turning down good opportunities for short-term sales when bars weren't right for us.

Over time, I would occasionally witness what happened when we didn't discriminate. As we grew larger, we hired extraordinary salespeople, individuals who were so kind, empathetic, and enthusiastic that you just couldn't help but want to buy from them. Sometimes they were *too* good. A bar would buy a lot of cases, but after some initial interest from drinkers, demand for our product would flag. Our salespeople had the integrity to go back in and do a promotion to get staff and drinkers excited again, which resulted in a sales bump. But then sales would fall back down again, suggesting that our beer really wasn't right for the place. Maybe the place was a Budweiser bar whose patrons wanted cheaper beer and would *never* appreciate our product. Maybe it was an Irish bar where patrons drank Guinness and Bass and little else. By getting our beer in there, our salespeople were only frustrating the bar manager and investing an enormous amount of our time and money that would have been better spent elsewhere. We served everyone's interests by placing our beer in only well-chosen spots. That in turn required considerably more thought, effort, and discipline on our part while we were doing the initial selling.

Once we found a bar that was a good match for our product, the next task was to persuade bar management that serving Samuel Adams was in their best long-term interest. Our conversation went something like this: "Look, Samuel Adams is a better beer than Heineken, and it costs you 25 cents more per bottle at wholesale. Do you think you could charge the drinker 50 cents more for a better beer?" If they said they thought they could, then I continued: "So if you charge a 50-cent premium per bottle, you'll make $6 extra on every case of Samuel Adams you sell. If you sell five cases a week, that's $30 a week and $1,500 a year added to your bottom line. And at the same time, you're offering your customer a higher-quality product. Do you think you have customers who would enjoy a beer like this? Doesn't that make sense?"

Sometimes they said yes. Mostly they didn't. Rejection was inevitable on a majority of occasions, and it was always hard to swallow. But I found it invigorating to discover that sales wasn't just about delivering a pitch; it was about having a meaningful conversation and doing a lot of listening. In trying to find customers for my beer, I was providing a real service—helping a customer understand and run their business better while having faith that in the end we would win, too. What could be better than that?

16

MY BEST SALES CALL
OF ALL TIME

JUST BECAUSE I SAW sales as a respectable pursuit didn't mean my customers were going to show me respect in turn. One late summer afternoon in 1985, I was calling on a Boston bar that I thought should carry Samuel Adams. I walked in after the lunch rush and found that the bar was almost empty. This was a good sign, because the manager wouldn't be able to say he was too busy to see me. I asked the bartender if the manager was around. "Oh, no," he said, understanding that I was there to sell something. "He's not here during the day. He's only here on Thursday nights."

"Okay, I can come back Thursday. When is a good time?"

"He generally comes in around nine thirty at night. If you come after ten, you might catch him."

I heard this a lot. It was a way of screening out salespeople who weren't really serious. A salesperson for a regular beer distributor was not going to show up at ten on a Thursday night. But I would, because this was my livelihood. No sales, no business.

I came in Thursday night at ten. The bartender, surprised, pointed around the corner. "He's downstairs. You'll see his office at the bottom of the staircase."

I headed down to find the manager sitting in a tiny office facing the stairs. He was "doing his bank," as it's called, taking all the cash and credit card receipts and matching them to the register tapes to make sure everything added up. He probably had a thousand dollars of cash on his desk. He heard me coming down the steps.

"Hi there," I said, but no sooner did I say it than I saw a little black circle facing me. My potential customer had a gun pointed right at my face. "Who the hell are you and what are you doing down here?"

I was stunned. "Uh, it's like, well . . ." It's hard to concentrate with a gun pointed at your face.

He didn't take the beer, but at least I escaped without getting shot. I decided right then that this was my best sales call of all time. From then on, no matter how badly it went, I could tell myself that at least nobody had pulled a gun on me.

That was put to the test a couple of years later when we were entering the New York City market. I was making the rounds in Greenwich Village with one of the distributor's salespeople. Sweet guy, great attitude, terrible salesperson. I was pumped, though, to be in New York. The Big Apple. If you can make it here, you can make it anywhere. For our first call of the day, we chose a brand-new place, an independent bar that had just opened. I thought it would be great to have Samuel Adams in this trendy new bar in this trendy part of Manhattan.

The bar's office was on the basement level. It was ten in the morning as I walked down the steps. We opened the door to find a woman at a table, doing paperwork. Obviously, she was either the owner or the manager.

"Hello!" I said, holding out my hand and cracking a friendly smile.

The woman looked up and scowled at me. "What do you want, fuckface?"

Not the greeting I expected. The only thing I could think of to say in response was, "That would be Mr. Fuckface to you."

That got a laugh out of her. Not that it helped my cause. She didn't take my beer. Still, she didn't point a gun at me. It was a good sales call.

YOU CAN'T HEAR WITH SOMEONE ELSE'S EARS

IN THE LATE SUMMER of 1985, as we were nearing a hundred accounts, I received a call from Atlas, a beer distributor that covered towns west of Boston in the Worcester, Massachusetts, area. The government mandated the creation of distributors in the wake of Prohibition, under what is known as the "three-tier system." With few exceptions, the law prohibited producers of alcoholic beverages from selling directly to licensed liquor establishments (fortunately, the law in Massachusetts has an exception, and we could serve as our own distributor). When I started Boston Beer, I would guess there were more than four thousand beer wholesalers in the United States. Today, there are fewer than fifteen hundred, owing to the consolidation of the mega-breweries. The system has its benefits and a few drawbacks, but it has survived for many very good reasons. Today, some of the industry's most financially successful people are wholesalers for beer, wine, and spirits.

The owner of Atlas had been fielding requests from bars and restaurants for Samuel Adams. He asked if Atlas could sign on as our first distributor. I was happy, though not entirely convinced. Aside from the fact that our product required intense personal effort to sell, it had a distinctly Bostonian name and heritage. Would we have what it took to sell our beer outside the immediate Boston area? Could Sam Adams sell as far away as Worcester, some fifty miles away?

I decided to find out. With Rhonda overseeing our existing accounts, I went out to Atlas's office and had a kick-off meeting with their sales team. For a few weeks, I rode with salespeople, investigated the key bars and restaurants, called on accounts—the same things we had been doing. I sensed right away that I needed to approach distributors as I did our customers, by seeing them as human beings and trying to understand their needs. And I should clarify: I'm not talking about strictly business needs. With both customers and distributors, I wanted to go beyond financial self-interest, getting them emotionally involved and "on our side." If I could do that, Samuel Adams would become more to them than just another brand in their selling materials. And in the case of distributors especially, we needed to be more than that because our volumes were so low. Distributors weren't making much money on Samuel Adams (even taking into account our higher margins), so they would only push Samuel Adams if they *cared* about the brand.

My intuition told me that Atlas would care if I just told them what my beer was all about. The leadership team at Atlas, probably like people at most distributors, saw their jobs as pretty straightforward. It was about getting the trucks out, keeping the costs down, keeping volume stable or increasing. None of the big brewers were coming to see them, talking about a loftier vision. They were just saying, "Here's your margin, let me take your order." I had a natural advantage because of my great passion for my product and my status as an underdog. As I told Atlas, Samuel Adams wasn't just a great beer; it represented a new way of thinking about beer. We were going to change the business by making great beer here in the United States and by upgrading people's taste in beer. We were going to do it together, against tremendous odds, in an industry overwhelmingly stacked against the little guy.

Within a few weeks, I got another phone call from Atlas. "Jim, we'd like to place an order. Can you send us a truckload of your beer?"

What?! A whole truckload?

"Sure, no problem," I responded.

A single brew represented four thousand cases, almost four truckloads, so we had enough beer to work with. Still, the scale of the order floored me. In six weeks, I had sold barely a truckload. Now I had sold one with a single phone call, notching $5,000 in profit (remember, these are 1985 dollars). This was big, a whole new league for us. We didn't have sophisticated systems to track our invoices; lacking computers and other back-office equipment (not to mention an office!), we couldn't even generate a professional-looking invoice. I wound up writing out the invoice myself by hand on a piece of stationery.

Getting Atlas on board didn't immediately solidify our business. We needed distributors' boots on the ground if we were to expand, but Atlas still couldn't do all of our high-touch selling for us. No matter how much we coaxed and inspired them, most of Atlas's sales force couldn't invest the kind of time to sell three cases of Samuel Adams a week when they could much more easily take an order for fifty cases of Miller Lite. It's tough to fight simple economics. In addition, their sales force didn't have the firsthand brewing expertise to sell our product—the deep knowledge of the brewing process and the ingredients, not to mention the passion for our bolder, higher-quality beer.

In general, beer distributors at the time weren't doing nearly as much as we were then to sell *anyone's* product. They were providing a vital service by storing large quantities of beer in warehouses, servicing customers, and keeping track of inventory. But the sales efforts of most distributors were often lackluster, especially at the point-of-sale. The breweries would send coasters, posters, table tents, and other promotional materials, but since salespeople at distributors didn't get paid to put that stuff up, it was a nuisance. I hate to say it, but from what people told me, point-of-sale materials often ended up in the Dumpster.

During the first summer after we launched, a man named Leonard Goldstein called and left a message on our answering service. At the time, Goldstein was CEO of Miller, the nation's second-largest brewery. I knew his name, and when I saw the 414 area code designating Milwaukee, Wisconsin, I thought, *It can't be.* Then I thought, *Uh-oh, did I do something to piss this guy off?* Turned out I had. When I called him back, he said, "Jim, I'm a Boston guy, and wherever I go, I look around in bars. I was in Faneuil Hall recently. In every bar I went into, I saw your goddamned table tents. I hear your company is just you and some broad. I want to know what you're doing that I'm not doing. I print lots of table tents. Millions of them. We're a big brewery and you're a start-up. What's the deal?"

I was stunned. "Well, honestly, Mr. Goldstein, we just put them up."

"What do you mean you just put them up?"

"Just what I said. I know you guys make lots of table tents, and as near as I can tell, the salesmen throw them away as soon as they get them. Or they put them in their trunk and drive around for a week or two, and then they throw them away. So that's what we're doing that you guys aren't. We're putting them up."

It was a thrill to know that I had caught the attention of someone like Leonard Goldstein, and it brought home to me the surprising advantage we had in our ground game. The big breweries might have reach through advertising, but we could offer better sales support because we didn't have to execute through as many layers as they did. Unfortunately for large brewers, the guy selling their products on the street was the person who cared least. At our company, it was the person who cared the most.

It was settled: Rhonda would cover Boston, and I would continue in Worcester and the surrounding area, working side by side with Atlas to educate customers and push the craft beer revolution forward, one area code at a time. Later in the year, when distributors from Hartford, Connecticut, and the Merrimack Valley in Massachusetts called, we did the same thing. Thus was born the basic strategy we would follow for a decade to achieve national distribution. In any local or regional market, Rhonda or I (and later our salespeople) would wait until a distributor called wanting to do business; that to us was a sign that demand existed in the local market where it really counted: with end drinkers. When a distributor approached, we talked to them and also approached other local distributors, picking one with whom we wanted to do business. We worked with our chosen distributor to develop customers and to maintain accounts in the territory even as the novelty of our product wore off. I personally would return to a territory as often as I could to work with problem accounts and keep distributors excited about our products. So much for a job that would keep me close to Boston!

Today we have four hundred professionals around the country who spend the great majority of their time going into bars and working with our customers. They're the best sales force in the industry—bright, educated individuals who have an expert's knowledge of our products, and, in many cases, experience as home brewers. In my role as chairman, I'm still out there, too, averaging a day or two a week working markets around the country. When I eat in a restaurant that serves Samuel Adams, I'll ask the server to tell me about the beer, so that I can understand what drinkers hear when they're trying to make their purchase decision. Sometimes at a bar I'll see someone drinking one of our competitor's beers and engage him or her in conversation. "I notice you're drinking a Corona. Have you ever tried Sam Adams? What did you think of it?"

If you want to run a successful business, you have to stay connected with people even as the business grows. There's some learning to be had reading market reports or watching focus groups behind a one-way mirror, but the best learning comes from interacting with users of your product and partnering closely with distributors and retailers. You can't leave it to others to sell your product while you run the company. Nobody knows, understands, or cares about your product the way you do. And nobody can proclaim its value to the world in all its greatness and glory the way you can.

People think a $200,000 market research report is good quality data—better, in any case, than sharing a beer with a few customers. I'd take a beer with my customers any day. The research company's report was probably written by an analyst who the day before was researching ladies' lingerie, and the day before that worked on deodorant. What do they know about beer? Not to mention you're not seeing the real data; you're seeing it in digested form. The analyst looked at the raw data and spit out a generic description of it, so it has lost its initial character. It began as food and you're getting it as barf. I want real food!

It takes skill and attention to listen to someone, to notice what they're really saying. We tend to think communication is just rhetoric—words strung together in persuasive ways. But people also communicate between the lines. They seem to be saying one thing when in fact they're saying four different things, talking about their fears and joys and hopes. I'd much rather hear it with my own ears and puzzle it out rather than trust the job to someone else. It takes artful listening to arrive at any useful insight.

Getting out there and putting ourselves in a position to do that listening has helped us again and again. A great early example was our decision to sell beer in kegs, not just bottles. I was in Legal Sea Foods in Cambridge, Massachusetts, talking to Billy the bartender. He was selling Harpoon on draft and had Sam in the bottles. I asked him how much Harpoon he sold, and he told me it was his slowest draft line—about a keg or two a week. And how much Sam Adams did he sell? "Oh, that sells really well," he told me, "it's one of my best bottled beers. About five cases a week." I did the math in my head:

A keg is equal to seven cases of bottled beer. So he was selling the equivalent of seven to fourteen cases of Harpoon, his slowest draft line. And his best bottled beer was only five cases. We needed to get into draft!

An even bigger piece of learning concerned our messaging. In the beginning, I described Samuel Adams with the phrase "America's Only Classic Lager" on our hangtags, emphasizing the notion that I was bringing back an original recipe for beer and resurrecting classic American beer. While this was certainly true, I realized over the course of thousands of barroom conversations that the message wasn't clicking. People liked how our beer tasted, yet they saw the imports as way more classic or historic than anything in America could be. What good was a nineteenth-century recipe against one that had been created in the fifteenth century? Heck, beer in Europe went back to the days of ancient Rome!

I needed a better explanation, one that would open people's hearts and minds to an American microbrewed beer. Months passed, and I couldn't crack it. One day, I was talking to a guy who was a die-hard Heineken drinker. I was trying to get him to drink Samuel Adams and he wasn't having it. "How can your beer be any good?" he asked. "It's American. Everything in America is mass-produced by robots."

"No, no," I said. "This beer is made in small batches. By human beings who really care about the beer. Like me. I do it myself, throw the hops into the kettle at just the right moment. This is my beer. I'm proud of it. Taste it."

That got his attention. "You're saying you pay attention to every single batch of beer?"

"Absolutely. The batches aren't that big and we make them one at a time. We make sure that everything is done the way it's supposed to be done. I hand-select the ingredients. They're the best in the world. And I taste a sample from every batch myself."

That did it. When he heard the words, "the beer is handcrafted in small batches," he was persuaded. He now understood why Samuel

Adams stood apart from the imports and the mass-produced American beers. An American beer that was handcrafted in small batches just felt good, evoking honest labor and a craftsperson who put his heart into the beer.

"Sounds like it's almost handmade," he said. And he ordered a Sam Adams.

I kept talking to drinkers, and repeatedly I saw that what they most responded to was the notion of a beer made by a passionate individual, someone who cared enough to ensure that every batch was perfect. Drinkers could accept that a beer that was "handcrafted in small batches" was better than the imports and they could justify paying a little more. The story of my family and the nineteenth-century recipe helped my cause, but it was this larger frame of careful, old-style, smaller-scale production that connected emotionally.

In 1986, two years after starting up, we changed our table tents to read "handcrafted in small batches," putting that phrase both on our labels and on materials delivered at the point-of-sale. Coupled with my public identity as an upstart and the scourge of stale imported beer (I'll talk even more about that), this phrase crystallized the identity of Samuel Adams Boston Lager as a flag bearer for other craft-brewed beers that were just then beginning to come onto the market. It was the first time the term "craft" had been applied to what was then called "microbrewing." Eventually, we would become known as a leader of the "craft beer movement." All from listening to a guy in a bar.

18

YOU DON'T CLIMB A MOUNTAIN TO GET TO THE MIDDLE

SHORTLY AFTER OUR LAUNCH, realizing we were going to radically exceed my initial goal of selling five thousand barrels a year within five years, we determined that we needed a new, loftier goal to aim for. I'm not big on having many goals, but I do think it's important for start-ups to have one, central goal. This goal should be challenging, but feasible; there's no point aiming for something impossible. I mentioned this to Rhonda one day as we sat at a bar in Boston's Faneuil Hall. "Rhonda, this is a mountain we're climbing, and no one climbs a mountain to get to the middle."

She looked at me funny. "What the hell does that mean?"

I took a look at the thick, creamy foam atop my glass of Sam. "It means we'll never compete with the Buds, the Millers, the Strohs, and the Coors of this world. But we need to take on the imports full force. Let's make the top of our mountain be the largest and most respected 'better beer' in America. Let's aim to outsell all the imports." I didn't say "premium beer," because in the beer industry, "premium" means cheap. Budweiser had called itself "premium" to distinguish itself from even cheaper, lower-quality brands. And

Michelob called itself "super premium" to indicate that it was better and higher-priced than Bud. What was better than super premium? Samuel Adams was, so lacking any other superlative, I called it "better beer."

Rhonda took a long sip of her beer. "I don't know, Jim. Outselling the imports? Is that realistic?"

I told her I thought it was. Not that year, maybe not in the next five years. Heck, it might take us fifty years. But it was doable. The imports were scrimping on quality to boost profits; they were trading on what had become an empty reputation and so were vulnerable. Heineken, for instance, wasn't using hops in their beer anymore but a cheaper extract from hops, which doesn't give beer the same complex bitterness. Cleaner and sharper, but much less flavorful. When we went into bars, we sometimes let drinkers compare real hops and their wonderful floral scent with hops extract, a dark liquid with a strong medicinal smell. There was no comparison; drinkers could tell the difference immediately. They were shocked, exclaiming, "You mean that's in my beer?!" Beyond using real hops, we were using distinguished and more expensive varieties of hops, Hallertau Mittelfrüh and Tettnang Tettnanger. We were also employing an old-fashioned brewing process that cost us more and produced more flavor.

If our beer was clearly better and if we had the best people working for us, why *couldn't* we eventually outsell the imports? Heineken had started from nothing in the United States fifty years earlier, and by 1985 they had a 1 percent share of the U.S. market, selling almost 2 million barrels a year. We could pull off something similar. I proposed that we would set ourselves a twenty-year goal: By 2005, we would outsell Heineken, the best-selling high-end beer. And if we didn't get there by 2005, we'd give ourselves another twenty years. As my girlfriend in high school told me, nothing good happens fast. I hated to hear that when I was sixteen, but she was right.

Rhonda agreed to the twenty-year goal, and from then on, we were determined to displace the imports as the best-selling and most respected beer in the United States. To make that goal stick, I hung a sign over my desk that read simply: "2005." Thirty years later, this remains our organizing objective. Everyone who joins our company is told from day one about this goal. It continues to galvanize us. We've made progress: Our sales have risen to over half of Heineken's. I know we'll get there one day.

GIVE THEM SOMETHING
TO TALK ABOUT

AS YOU GET YOUR start-up off the ground, a little publicity backing you up doesn't hurt. But how do you attain that publicity and sustain it over time, especially when you don't have much money?

During the first few months of Boston Beer's operations, I experienced firsthand the power of mass media advertising to build awareness around specific brands. One establishment, the St. Botolph Restaurant in Boston's Back Bay neighborhood, had flat out refused to sell my beer because I couldn't afford to advertise. "My customers don't drink beer," the manager told me. "They drink advertising. Come back when you can advertise." It was the very opposite of my father's dictum and an assertion I just couldn't accept.

Advertising had reach (the ability to hit a wide audience) and frequency (the ability to do that repetitively, so that people got and remembered the message). I could achieve reach using public relations, but if I wanted to achieve frequency, I would need to find ways to make news again and again and again. Some people who work with a public relations firm or consultant are content to write them a check each month and tell them, "Make me famous." That wouldn't work for us. I knew I would help my cause by feeding Sally, my PR consultant, a steady stream of newsworthy story hooks and angles. She had the contacts, knew how to work the media, and knew what sold, but as the entrepreneur, I had a unique ability and responsibility to find opportunities to snag journalists' attention. Some may call this scrappiness; I called it necessity.

Sally didn't create a press kit for us, such as many new companies have. Press kits make companies look bigger, more established. We didn't want to look bigger. We just wanted the media to report on who we were and what we were doing. We had three basic stories to work with: our "David versus Goliath" narrative as a tiny entrant into an industry dominated by the likes of Budweiser and Miller; my own story as a Harvard guy who risked everything to follow his passion; and the story of the historical figure of Samuel Adams. Our media outreach strategy was simple: Don't turn anybody away. Take whatever publicity we can get. And always look for more.

We got a few stories out around the time Samuel Adams Boston Lager first hit Boston's bars and restaurants, but nothing too earth-shaking; *People* magazine had put us off, saying, "Sorry, we don't break trends; we follow them."

Okay. . . .

Fortunately for us, our profile was about to get bigger. In June 1985, Sally, Rhonda, and I flew to Denver to compete in the Fourth Annual Great American Beer Festival. Picture nearly a thousand beer lovers milling around a noisy old ballroom at the Regency Hotel, some pouring beer, others drinking it. More than a hundred different beers were being served from brewers big and small across America—everyone from Budweiser and Miller to regional brands like Narragansett and Genesee to a few nascent microbrewed beers like Mendocino Brewing Company and New Amsterdam. Attendees received a ballot on the stub of their tickets letting them vote for their favorite beer.

At about 10 P.M., the lights dimmed. Daniel Bradford, one of the festival founders, took the microphone to announce the winners of the Great American Beer Festival. I took a deep breath and glanced at Rhonda, who was standing behind our little section of a large, double horseshoe–shaped arrangement of tables. "You ready for this?"

She nodded.

"In tenth place . . . ," Daniel said.

We held our breath as he identified the beer.

It wasn't us.

A smattering of applause and cheering rippled through the crowd.

"In ninth place . . . ," Daniel said.

Again we held our breath.

Again it wasn't us.

"That's okay," I said. "Don't worry."

But I was a little worried. For Rhonda and me, this was about validation. The best brewers in the country were here. This was their first chance to taste my beer. It would mean a lot to us to know that they liked and respected what were doing. It was why Rhonda was wearing her "lucky dress." It was why we spent the money for the plane tickets, the hotel rooms, the entrance fee, and the cost of shipping our beer to Denver.

Eighth place.

Still not us.

Seventh place. Sixth place. Fifth place.

Still not us.

Now I felt butterflies in my stomach.

The countdown continued. Fourth place—not us. Third place—not us. Second place—not us.

Oh, crap.

My hopes were fading. I thought how cool it would've been to place in the top ten. Yet the likelihood of placing had now fallen to an ungodly one in a hundred. Rhonda and I looked at each other and shrugged our shoulders.

Daniel stared down at the paper he had in his hand. "And now, I'm pleased to announce the top beer, as voted by attendees at this year's event. The winner is . . . Samuel Adams Boston Lager!"

A chill went down my spine. My heart practically stopped. What? We won? We won! Holy shit!!!

We had just been picked as the best beer in America by the brewers and drinkers in this country who knew and cared most about beer. Nobody had ever heard of Samuel Adams, and yet we had just won the only big award in American beer.

Rhonda and Sally stayed at the table while I went up to collect our award. From behind the table they looked up and saw what looked like everyone in the room moving toward our table to taste the winning beer. Within a half-hour, we were totally out of beer. We didn't even save a six-pack for our own celebration afterward.

The morning after our victory, Sally, Rhonda, and I were at the airport, heading home, when we learned our flight had been delayed. We would be stuck in the terminal for several hours. We looked over and saw a carousel of pay phones—six of them arranged in a circle. In an era before cell phones, this was our ticket. Sally called *The Boston Globe*, told them about our award, and asked if they wanted to speak to me. While I was talking to them, she went to the next phone and called the Associated Press. When I finished up with the *Globe*, I talked to the Associated Press, and Sally went on to call WEEI, then the Boston news radio station. We went around the carousel like this, Sally half a phone call ahead of me.

Finally, our flight was called. For the next several hours, as we made our way back across America, Sally and I drafted a press release about the award—our first press release ever. When we arrived in Boston, we all shared a cab from the airport. The cabbie had news radio on. I'll never forget entering Sumner Tunnel and hearing the lead story: "In the news today, the Boston Beer Company, maker of Samuel Adams Boston Lager, was just named the best beer in America in Denver."

We cheered and laughed in the cab that afternoon. During the following weeks, many media outlets ran stories. It was a huge boost, a third-party endorsement exceeding all our expectations. And its effects were lasting. A couple of months later, having seen the buzz about us, *Inc.* magazine called, wanting to chat and maybe in the future do a story. The resulting article, "Portrait of the CEO as Salesman," related the same basic ideas about selling I'm recounting in this book. I'm told the article remains one of the top five most downloaded stories in the magazine's history.

A couple of months after the festival, in the summer of 1985, George Thaler, an investor and consultant at BCG, approached me, saying he thought he could find a market for Samuel Adams in Germany. George was an Austrian living in Munich at the time. Having become restless at BCG and seeing the initial success I was having, he wanted to start a part-time business distributing Samuel Adams there. I was happy to say yes. The added sales might be nice, but I had another idea: Could we get press coverage in the United States for selling beer in Germany? Everyone in the world understood that the Germans knew and cared about beer; heck, it was the national drink. If Germany as a country accepted our beer, that would be the third-party endorsement to end all third-party endorsements.

I brought the idea to Sally, and she agreed we should pursue it. It would be like "bringing coals to Newcastle," she said, referencing the old English saying about trying to sell coal to a town that already heavily exported it (in German the equivalent is "bringing olive oil to Athens"). George looked into what it would take administratively to export to Germany. It turned out we didn't have to do much—just pass Germany's traditional beer purity law, the *Reinheitsgebot.* That wasn't a problem. The Germans did try to keep us out at first, claiming they had found some strange protein additive not allowed by the law. I promptly dispatched Joe Owades, who explained to the German experts how the yeast (which we were allowed to use) had produced the protein itself. Thus we became the first American beer to be sold in Germany. I like to observe that at the same time we were looking into expanding into Connecticut, and it took more paperwork and red tape to send the beer to Connecticut than to get it into Germany!

We hired a public relations professional in Munich to tell our story. Weeks later she sent us a one-inch binder full of clippings about us in German newspapers and magazines. The German public had apparently been shocked to discover that Americans could brew really good beer; they had thought all we had in the ex–British colonies was the weaker, more watery stuff. I couldn't understand most of the stories, but one was easy to translate: "Ein Bier für Yuppies."

Stateside, we played on our presence in Germany by putting new hangtags on our beer reading, "America's Only Imported Beer." When you opened up the tag, the meaning became clear: "Imported into Germany." *Newsweek* magazine picked up the story, coincidentally adopting Sally's response as its title: "Coals to Newcastle."

If you haven't been proactively seeking out ways that your fledgling business can make news, it's time to start. Figure out the main PR angles, and proceed from there. Do something worth talking about. Aim for a superlative: Be the first, the best, the only, the biggest, the smallest. When we started, we were the "smallest brewer in America." Then we became known as the "best beer in America," then as the "only American beer in Germany." Today, we're the "largest craft brewer." All simple, memorable superlatives. What kinds of genuine news items can you come up with? What can you do to raise eyebrows? The world is dying to learn about your business and its story. They just don't know it yet.

20

WHEN YOU'RE RIGHT, PUSH IT

IN MAY 1986, about a year after our launch, Boston Beer Company did its first advertising. Sort of. No, I had not dispensed with my misgivings about marketing, but I had donated some beer to the Boston radio station WBCN for its Christmas party, and got offered free airtime in exchange (some of their spots were going unsold after midnight). Although our agency offered to write up an ad and have it produced using radio talent, I rejected this idea as expensive and time consuming (I'd have to keep track of how often the ad ran and pay the talent royalties, what were called "residuals"). Since we had our hands full brewing and selling beer, I figured I'd write and record the ad myself. I would keep it simple—just me talking about the beer. No music, no jocks, no girls. I was aware I didn't have special voice-over talent (someone once called Boston Beer Company and asked if I'd recorded the spots after my death), but nobody knew more about my beer or cared as much, and that had to count for something.

I decided to use the ad as an opportunity to take on foreign beers directly. Our biggest challenge with drinkers, I was realizing, was that we weren't making enough headway against the imports. Some drinkers had adopted our beer because they liked the taste and responded to elements of our story, but many others whom I met in bars said, "Well, Samuel Adams is good for an American beer, but it's not imported" or "The imports are masters of beer. Come back in a century when you've mastered it." It didn't matter if Heineken or Beck's tasted skunky in blind taste tests; many people thought skunky was what beer was supposed to taste like and were happy to stick with what they knew. The notion of a beer or anything else being "imported" had an ingrained cachet, suggesting luxury, sophistication, elegance, and quality that justified a higher price. If I couldn't somehow puncture this notion, I would never be able to take Samuel Adams beyond a certain point. We could win the bronze, but not gold.

It happened to be the one hundredth anniversary of the Statue of Liberty that year, so I incorporated an immigration theme into my messaging for the radio ad. The text went like this: "When we asked for Europe's tired and poor, we didn't mean their beer. They make great beer in Europe. But the beer they send us is hardly their best. Instead, they send us Beck's and St. Pauli Girl brewed lighter and less flavorful for America, with adjuncts not used in their European versions.* There are adjuncts in the Heineken we get, too. And those adjuncts keep all these beers from being sold in Germany; they're outlawed under the Germans' strict beer purity law." I ended with a line similar to one we were using on our hangtags: "So if you want to taste beer the way the great European brewers really make it, drink my Samuel Adams. Or drink in Europe."

With all the time I had been spending in bars talking about my beer, it felt right to get on the radio and transmit my same message to a wider audience. And it would continue to feel right. As we entered new markets, we announced our arrival with different versions of the radio ads. Today, we're still doing ads like this. But that first ad was special, sparking a controversy that put us in the national news.

---

* An adjunct is an ingredient like corn that gives the beer less flavor or texture, allowing it to be made at a lower cost.

Within weeks after my radio ads hit the Boston market, all hell broke loose. A range of media, including Boston newspapers, *Adweek*, and the Associated Press, picked up the story. Beck's and Heineken defended themselves, with Beck's denying that their beer on the American market contained adjuncts and Heineken brushing off the notion that adjuncts even mattered. I persisted for two reasons: I believed I was right, and I felt I was making an important statement about why my beer was better. Sally brought the story to Mark Starr, Boston bureau chief of *Newsweek*, and he liked the David versus Goliath angle. He filed a story declaring that Beck's, St. Pauli Girl, and Heineken were perpetrating a "sham, one of the last of the great consumer hoaxes."

Heineken announced that they weren't going to sue me, but I heard they were so upset with the *Newsweek* story that they permanently pulled their advertising from the magazine. Meanwhile, the sky above Boston went black with lawyers. I heard from attorneys representing Beck's, their importers, and even some of their distributors. These lawyers wrote letters threatening lawsuits unless I apologized and ran commercials correcting the slander I was alleged to have perpetrated. In the *Newsweek* article, a vice-president at the Beck's importer ominously remarked, "I would smell a lawsuit coming."

It's always a little nerve-wracking to get letters printed on the engraved letterhead of a big-deal New York law firm. I went to law school with these types. I knew that the jugular was their second favorite target.

Attacking the imports was a "bet the company" move, because losing a lawsuit would have ruined us. Here we were, a six-person, pipsqueak company, and we were directly attacking the fundamental advantage enjoyed by these huge imported brands. But I wasn't going to issue a retraction. I *knew* I was right. Before our ads ran, I had sent samples of Beck's, St. Pauli Girl, and Heineken to Germany to be tested by the authorities, and Heineken had come back as containing corn, a fact that the company's American importer acknowledged.

Beck's and St. Pauli Girl had passed the test, but I remained suspicious so I sent one of our employees, Walter Scheurle, to Germany to do a little extra low-key fact finding. He confirmed that the truth about the imports was much less attractive than it seemed.

Walter was a German brewmaster I met when he was working at Pittsburgh Brewing. He loved brewing Samuel Adams and said he wanted to work for us selling beer, so I hired him. His original expertise was in fluid dynamics; the United States had brought him over from Germany to help them model the effects of nuclear weapons on the human body. From there, Walter had gone on to work in the space program, and then in beer. I had thought it outlandish at first that a former engineer–turned-brewmaster could sell beer effectively, but Scheurle won me over. Not only were his traditional German looks straight out of central casting (think big apple cheeks, handlebar mustache, stout build, and jolly demeanor), but he had a deep passion for our beer and boundless energy.

Walter went over to the Beck's brewery in Bremen, telling employees there that he was working for us and asking for the professional courtesy of a brewery tour. Since the media frenzy had not yet broken out, Beck's brewmasters hadn't heard of us and didn't perceive us as a threat, so they said yes. At one point on the tour, Walter spotted a pipe going into a brew kettle. "What's that for?" he asked.

"Oh, that's the pipe we use for the *brau zucker* (beer sugar). It's for the Americans."

"Oh, really," Walter said.

BUSTED!

But Walter wasn't done yet. "You know, we might be interested to know more about the beer sugar. We're always interested in German ingredients."

The tour guide gave us the name of the supplier Beck's used. When we called the supplier and purchasing agents, they confirmed that Beck's was buying sugar to lighten the American version of their beer. And they told us how much. I don't remember the exact numbers, but these were large amounts—millions of pounds. All of this to produce lighter beer more cheaply for the innocent, unsuspecting American beer drinker.

This evidence was strong, so I went ahead even though it was essentially Walter's word against Beck's. I would later get definitive proof when a scientist at MIT named Rae Krueger called me up: "Mr. Koch, I've been reading about these beer wars. Your opponents might not know this, but we have a lab here that can test the beer to determine definitively if sugar was used in the brewing." Krueger explained that there are two distinct ways that photosynthesis occurs in plants, and that corn, sugarcane, pineapple, and a handful of other plants used a different pathway than grain. Using a test that was certified by the FDA, she could check for traces of both pathways, identifying with certainty whether corn or cane adjuncts had been used. She performed the test, and sure enough, Beck's, Heineken, and St. Pauli Girl all came back as containing adjuncts.

I now knew I was in the clear: The imports could threaten to sue me all they wanted, but they would be exposed in a court of law if they sued, so I knew they wouldn't. I continued to make my case at promotional tastings and in the media, and I didn't mince words. Over time, Heineken, Beck's, and St. Pauli Girl all changed their ingredients and recipes as a result of the pressure I was bringing to bear—a victory for beer drinkers. Still, scars from the battle took a while to heal, and perhaps they haven't entirely. In 1997, Philip Van Munching, a marvelous writer whose family's company imported Heineken into the United States, wrote a book called *Beer Blast*. It had a chapter titled "Sam Adams: Brewer, Patriot, Pain in the Ass," a play on the "Brewer, Patriot" moniker that appears on our bottles. In the chapter, Van Munching details our battles with the imports and remarks that his father, who ran Van Munching & Company at the time, "remains convinced that Jim Koch is the antichrist."

Nobody likes being called the antichrist, but I had been a little unorthodox and hit them in their vulnerable spot. In grade school there's always that kid who sits in front, takes diligent notes, puts his hand up first, chats up the teacher—and who is now a successful attorney or dentist. In taking on the imports, I proved to myself and others that being the kid in the back who made wisecracks and made people laugh was also a viable path to success. Almost overnight, I gained notoriety for helping to launch a craft beer revolution, with the media portraying me as the feisty underdog willing to stand up and take his shots.

I had dented the reputation of imported beer a little, and I would continue to chip away at it for the next three decades. No matter how long it took to convince American drinkers that a beer brewed in the United States offered higher quality, I would stay in the game. My love of better, more flavorful beer and my need to keep Boston Beer Company relevant to good beer drinkers demanded nothing less.

If you're going to try to create a revolution in an industry, as we were doing, you have to actually *be* a revolutionary. You have to make some enemies, maybe even be considered the antichrist. I would later get myself into trouble taking some stupid risks, but this time, I made the right choice. I put my neck out there and stirred people up, something the historical figure of Samuel Adams himself was so good at. And history proved me right.

TAKE THE GIANT TURDS IN STRIDE

GETTING INTO GERMANY, winning the Great American Beer Festival, getting our first distributors, learning how to sell—the first several years brought some exciting times. To this list I should add another thrill: getting our beer into the White House.

A friend of mine from BCG knew the buyer there, so I was able to arrange a meeting. I showed up, was buzzed in through the front gate, and got to tour the underground cafeteria, which they called "The White House Mess." Yes, there was an office in the White House labeled "The White House Mess." It was actually quite tidy inside. Learning that the Mess didn't stock high-end imported beers, only Stroh's, Miller, Coors, and the like, I pointed out that visitors and staff might like a flavorful beer brewed in America. "You know, Samuel Adams was a patriot and founder of the country, but he hasn't yet seemed to have made it to the White House. I think he'd be pleased to be here now." The buyer placed an order, which expanded to include Air Force One, Camp David, and the presidential box in the Kennedy Center. The distributor told me that the secret service came to their warehouse with a van to pick out exactly which cases the White House wanted. Pretty cool to have my beer being picked up by guys with earpieces and concealed weapons.

There was also the satisfaction that first year of taking on the trappings of a successful start-up. We hired a couple of drivers, one of whom, Dean Gianocostas, is still with us as a brewer and has starred in our TV commercials (he's the guy with salt-and-pepper hair who doesn't say much). We rented our first office, an attic right above Sally's office. It was the former servants' quarters of an old Boston mansion, and it came complete with a sloped roof, gables, and a claw-footed bathtub covered with a piece of plywood that I used as a desk. We got our first phone line and hired Jeannie Zucker, a very organized former BCG secretary, as our office manager. We started doing the kind of basic accounting stuff businesses do, like withholding social security for employees. I still wasn't taking a salary, but because of our bare-bones business plan, which kept fixed costs as low as possible, we had been profitable within the first month and stayed profitable.

It wasn't all good times. The first six months after our launch were challenging personally on account of the sheer amount of change I experienced. Gone was the structure of an office and a corporate job. Gone was my work with clients like GE. Gone were my old home and family life. My wife Susan and I split up as I was launching the company, and I moved into an apartment with no furniture. We shared custody of our two children, and my times with them were sacred and created some structure to my weeks. Every day was a blank sheet of paper that I filled in with activities required to move the business forward. My life became far less certain, less stable, less corporate, and more improvisational. Also, with all the sales calls, trainings, and promotional events I did, it became more nocturnal. All this was invigorating, but something to get used to. Change is good, I reminded myself.

As far as the business itself went, there were anxious moments when sales seemed to stall, leaving me to wonder: *Is this it? Is this as big as we'll get?* I just had no idea how many people would want to drink our beer. Sales did wind up rising again, a pattern that would repeat itself several times during our first ten years of rapid growth.

We ran into problems as well with our early hires. I was at a bar one day and spotted a guy drinking Bass Ale. I saw this as a perfect opportunity to convert him to my beer. "So, I notice you're drinking a Bass," I said. "I've heard good things about that beer, but have you ever tried Sam Adams?"

"Oh, yeah," he said, "I love that beer."

"How come you're not drinking it?"

"Because I get it all the time for free."

That got my attention. "Really, you get it for free?"

He grinned. "Yeah. I've got a source in the company who gets me beer."

It took all my effort to restrain myself. I had known that some of our beer was going missing, but I didn't know how it was happening. "Wow. Maybe I could get some. What company do you work for?"

He told me the name of a temporary employment service we used when we needed extra drivers to deliver our beer. It turned out one of their drivers was giving our beer away and also selling some of it at a 50 percent discount to accounts, pocketing the cash himself. All because we had no inventory control.

I fired him along with a second driver who turned out to be selling drugs—a decision that came back to haunt us, Jeannie in particular.

Jeannie was a cheerful young woman of Scandinavian descent, much more serious-minded than the typical twentysomething. One day, she walked in to find the door to her office open and . . . how can I put this delicately . . . a large but not quite steaming pile of shit on her desk. (I am not making this up.)

She started screaming. "Jim! Jim! Sally's dog pooped on my desk."

I shot her a disbelieving look. "Sally's dog couldn't get up on your desk even if he wanted to." She had a forty-pound standard poodle named Spot; he wasn't about to make a three-foot vertical jump.

"Well, someone's dog pooped on my desk."

I took a look. There it was: a giant turd. "It's not Spot's," I said, keeping my distance. Then it dawned on me. That wasn't a dog turd. That was a human turd.

We later figured out that this noxious discovery was a going-away present from that driver, who still had a key to the office. Many people in the working world have a metaphorical pile of shit on their desks. Jeannie had a real one.

As bad as a disgruntled employee is, there are worse things a newbie entrepreneur has to deal with, like getting arrested. During the fall of 1985, a buddy and I went climbing for a day on Cannon Mountain in New Hampshire. We were traveling light, just a rope, some climbing equipment, a couple of water bottles, and candy bars. As we climbed higher and higher, we found that the terrain was wet, so we had to go off the route, costing us time. By the time we got to the top, it was dark. The temperature was probably in the high forties and the wind was blowing.

We weren't that far from civilization; Cannon Mountain Ski Resort was located on the backside of this peak. But we couldn't find the trail down in the darkness, and I wasn't about to stumble around at the top of an eight-hundred-foot cliff.

We could make out the flickering lights of a small lodge at the top of the mountain where the ski lift ended, so we headed there to check if anyone was around who could help us. The doors were locked, but I spotted a pay phone inside. We rapped on the window for someone to let us in, making as much noise as we could. Nobody came. After twenty minutes of knocking and banging on the door, I had had enough and I decided I needed another solution. I picked up a rock and broke a windowpane, reached in, and opened the door. No sooner were we inside than a man appeared. He wasn't armed, but he was mad as hell. It was eight o'clock at night—what were we doing here?

I tried to explain our situation, but he didn't want to hear it. He started up the lift and told us we could ride to the bottom. When we got there, the police were waiting. They took us to the station and booked us for burglary, trespassing, breaking and entering, and malicious destruction of property before releasing us on our own recognizance. This was serious: Burglary was a felony, and I had just applied for a license to sell beer in New Hampshire. If I was convicted, it could prevent Boston Beer Company from expanding into New Hampshire and probably cause problems in other states.

Fortunately, the district attorney dropped the charges (the law allows you to damage property if you are in physical danger, so he didn't have much of a case). I paid to replace the window; it cost me $50, glazier and all. Having the charges dropped protected me with the Liquor Control Board, since you had to be convicted of a felony for the board to hold up a license. As it turned out, the board delayed action on my application anyway—apparently they had discretion to do that—but they eventually relented.

It was a close call, and an illustration of how fragile young companies are. All the hard work I put into Boston Beer Company could have been undone in an instant because of a stupid climbing miscalculation, my desire not to take chances in the dark on top of a mountain, and breaking a $50 window. I knew that competition in the beer industry was tough, but it had never occurred to me that mortal dangers to a company could come from outside the business world. So much of a company's success is luck—the opportunities you were able to grasp when they came along, the unforeseen dangers you managed to avoid. Shit happens, you just have to accept it.

That's not to say you should adopt a passive, fatalistic attitude. Lots of opportunities in business are *made*, not stumbled upon. The key is to scrap around and create your desired reality as best you can.

Here's a quick example. Clarendon Wine Co. is a highly visible Back Bay liquor store, and I really wanted them to carry Samuel Adams. It was located right around the corner from our office, so I walked by every day. When I made a sales call there, the manager said, "Jeez, I'd love to carry your beer, but I don't get any calls for it. If

I place an order, it'll just sit here and get stale. Tell you what. I'll call you if I get any customer requests."

That night, I noticed that I had accumulated a couple of cases of empty bottles in the back of my car. The light bulb went off. *I wonder if this would work . . .*

Rather than returning the empties to the brewery, I left them at various places in the alley behind Clarendon Wine Co. Sure enough, enterprising homeless people, known as recycling entrepreneurs, picked them up, brought them around the corner, and redeemed them in the store. All of a sudden, the manager was seeing all these Samuel Adams bottles come back; to him, it must have looked as if everyone was suddenly drinking this hot new beer.

The homeless people in the neighborhood got a little extra change. And it wasn't long before we had a new account.

In general, I coped with all the setbacks and the change by immersing myself in work. I tolerated the giant turds, the near disasters, and the unsteady sales because I had committed myself wholeheartedly to my new venture. I advise that you do the same. Don't second-guess yourself. Don't panic. Just stay the course.

In rock climbing, when you start out on a certain route, you say that you're "committed." You're far enough off the ground that it's easier to keep climbing up than to try to climb back down. All that matters is what's ahead of you, so you don't worry, and you don't look down. Nothing good happens from looking down. Look up and find the next handhold and the next foothold and the one after that. You keep going. You trust yourself, even when you can't see the whole path in front of you. If I could survive my own embarrassing screw-ups and keep going, then you can, too.

PART III

FERMENTING

(1988-1995)

When the wort is cool, add the yeast. Give these tiny organisms time to break down the sugars in the wort into carbon dioxide and alcohol. Fermentation is magical and mysterious, just like the growth of a start-up. We may understand about strategy, operations, finance, or sales, but who ultimately knows by what alchemy a successful company is made?

22

GROW SKINNY

ONE MONDAY MORNING in 1988, three years after our launch, I was in the car on my way to work when I realized something: *I have no idea where the company is . . .*

With business growing every month, Jeannie had found us a new, bigger space. The moving date had been the previous Friday. I had been on the road all that week, and although I remembered signing a lease, I was so busy brewing and selling beer that I didn't quite register the address. I had literally lost my company. I knew it had to be somewhere near that attic over Sally's office, but I didn't have a clue where it had gone.

I called Jeannie from my car phone. What followed was a slightly embarrassing conversation, not unlike the one I had with Rhonda after making our first sale. "Uh, Jeannie, where are we?"

"What do you mean?" she asked.

"I mean, we moved, right? Where did we go?"

There was a stunned silence on the line. "We're in the Paine Furniture Building, Jim. At the corner of Arlington Street and St. James Avenue."

"What floor?"

"It's the fifth floor, Jim. Are you okay?"

Jeannie probably wondered if I was "all there," and not without reason. On other occasions, I had come into the office after forgetting to shut off my car. Each time, I had been parked outside, talking on my car phone, and because I was so engrossed in the call, I just got out of the car and walked away. Eventually pedestrians saw the Boston Beer Company lettering on the side of the car (I was still delivering beer, so I had commercial plates) and called us: "Uh, yeah, I don't know whose car this is, but I walked past it a couple of hours ago and it was running. It's still running and there's nobody in it." Once, nobody called and the car kept running until it ran out of gas. It was so stupid that all I could do was laugh and wait for AAA.

Other entrepreneurs may identify with my disorientation. The growth of our company was overwhelming. Our revenues were expanding at an average of 50 percent a year during the late 1980s. Our company doubled in size every eighteen months. We were perpetually being forced to perform our operations at a scale we'd never anticipated. By 1990, we had thirty employees and were hiring more each month as we opened markets in new cities and states (we also opened a Samuel Adams Brewhouse in Philadelphia, in partnership with Philadelphia restaurateur David Mink). We were in thirty-three states by the end of that year, selling 115,000 barrels a year—6 million six-packs. During the following year, 1991, the country was hit by a severe recession but our sales were still up 48 percent, increasing to 173,000 barrels. By 1992, we were available in forty-nine states and five foreign countries, selling a whopping 275,000 barrels. We claimed about 30 percent market share among America's 150 craft breweries and were the first craft-brewed beer to achieve nearly nationwide distribution.

We were able to handle this rapid and intense growth without any major disasters for a number of reasons. First, we weren't pursuing a "growth at all costs" strategy, rushing to "own" markets before our competitors could. People frequently told me that I was in a race to "own" the craft beer market before someone else did, but I didn't really believe that. Many companies mess themselves up believing they have to "own the market" before competition does. In truth, it usually takes competition longer than you think to crop up because it's hard to duplicate a business and get it right. And if you keep moving forward deliberately, competition has an even harder time catching you. So we continued to pursue *organic* growth, opening up new markets once wholesalers started calling us from these markets, indicating that potential demand existed. This allowed us time to promote people from within rather than hire professional management from the outside, ensuring we could maintain our culture. Growth was challenging for us at times, but it was never something we couldn't accommodate.

Second, our model was simple and scalable. Since we were contract brewing our beer, we didn't need to invest a lot of capital in order to expand our production. As a result, we never needed to borrow money or bring in any more investors (when the money people come in, the culture of an organization inevitably changes). The raw ingredients we needed to brew our beer—grain, hops, water, yeast—were readily available on the market in sufficient quantity. I could still taste a bottle from every batch. The main investment we had to make in order to ramp up was hiring more salespeople, as well as a few others to provide support. And as I've mentioned, we ignored marketing people entirely and didn't hire our first marketing person until late 1994, when we were already into our second decade.

Third, I was willing to offload work to other people. As an entrepreneur, it's easy to fall into the trap of believing you are better at any given job than somebody you might hire. This belief might hold true for a while, but eventually it impedes the growth of the company, the people, and even the founder. You need to figure out pretty quickly what you can and want to offload to others. If the company is growing

60 percent in a year, your job is also growing 60 percent a year—and you probably don't have 60 percent more time. You need to get rid of 60 percent of your job every year. I decided by the late 1980s that I would focus my time on just a few key things: the quality of the beer, the quality of the people, and our culture. Everything else, I delegated to other people.

This brings me to Rhonda, a fourth factor behind our successful growth. She had excellent business acumen, and by the late 1980s she held primary responsibility for all our salespeople. This critical and demanding job had Rhonda staying up late each night reading call reports from our sales team and traveling most of the time to make sales calls herself (she eventually bought a condo near the airport to make her travels more manageable). Rhonda was a natural leader, not just because of her energy, drive, and willingness to work extraordinarily hard, but because of her ability to stay grounded. To her, everything came down to people. She motivated everyone on our sales force to do their best, helped to standardize our practices for hiring and training new salespeople, and managed them once they were in the field. Having someone as smart, dedicated, and trustworthy as Rhonda left me free to handle other parts of the business that required close attention.

A fifth and final reason we were able to expand without growing ourselves out of business goes back to my String Theory. We provisioned ourselves with the resources we absolutely needed to grow, but we were also very good at challenging ourselves to make do with less. So many big companies add layers upon layers of people as they grow. A few years later they realize that they've gotten too big so they have this big purge, laying people off and giving it a fancy name like "rightsizing" or "reengineering the workforce." After that, they grow some more and eventually hire more people. This lurching from overeating to crash dieting seems like an extremely unhealthy path to growth. I say don't hire people if you're going to lay them off in a few years. It's morally wrong. It's also expensive (often requiring that an entrepreneur in the early stages give up equity) and it damages morale. Don't hire until employees will pay for themselves, either in more sales or cost savings, on day one.

If you have a problem to solve, the *least* efficient way to solve it is to hire someone. Let's say you hire someone, and that person during the course of their day has to coordinate and interact with five existing employees. That interaction may take up, say, 5 percent of the time of each of those five people, making them each 5 percent less efficient. So you've added one person, but really you're only adding 75 percent of a person. That new person takes 10 percent of his or her manager's time, too; since the manager makes 50 percent more in salary, you've lost another 15 percent of the value added by the new employee, bringing you down to 60 percent. Then, you add in the incremental cost of the extra support systems you have to have as you add more people—accounting, human resources, and so on. Ultimately, you may only be looking at getting 50 percent or less of a new hire's time in net value—but you're paying 100 percent of his or her salary. If you can find a way to make do with fewer people, you're going to be much better off.

That kind of discipline isn't easy, but there are tricks you can try. For instance, find a great office location that is a convenient commute for everyone (which also enables you to draw from a larger talent pool), but keep your space small, giving employees just enough room to do their job efficiently. I always did this, taking a cue from what I had seen at BCG, where the consultants shared offices. It boils down to human psychology. If employees see no empty space, they're going to think, *Hmm, we don't have room to hire someone else. How can we make do with what we already have?* But if they are spread out amid empty cubicles, they're going to think, *Hmm, we have room for more people, and we have lots of work to do, so we should really be filling these cubicles up.* Scarcity spawns invention, and invention is precisely what any company needs. So, to anyone who has started a company and is experiencing some initial success, keep it skinny as you grow. I might not have known where my office was that morning in 1988, but I could rest assured that we had pared it down to what we absolutely needed in order to keep growing at 60 percent a year. We had workspace—not ego space.

23

IF YOU'RE NOT THE LEAD DOG, THE SCENERY NEVER CHANGES

WHEN YOU'RE SUCCESSFUL in any industry, eventually you will have competition. During the late 1980s ours came from dozens and eventually hundreds of emerging craft beers. We had a formula for small brewing that seemed to work. Observing how much fun we were having, a number of amateur businesspeople, brewers, and beer lovers wanted in—from Wolfgang Puck to a urologist in Atlanta. The result was a renaissance in brewing, with some 250 commercial breweries opening in the United States by 1990. New brands flew onto store shelves, including fly-by-night names like Bad Frog, Lucky Kat, Brewski, Wicked Ale, and Rhino Chasers, and more enduring ones like Brooklyn Lager and Fat Tire. Although microbrews still comprised only 3 percent of the overall beer market, the frenzy of activity was enough to make an impression on Fritz Maytag, who, as I wrote earlier, had acquired the Anchor Brewing Company in 1965. He was considered by many to be "the father of microbrewing," and had inspired me in my own venture. "I'm just bamboozled," he told *Time* magazine in 1987. "It's astonishing to see the number of breweries and brands."

As a lover of better beer, I was thrilled to see craft brewing catching on. What *did* bother me was the harsh tone some early competitors took. A few craft brewers grew jealous of us and instead of focusing on building themselves up, tried to tear us down by smearing us in the media and tarnishing our accomplishments. We heard grumbling about our contract brewing arrangements, as if they somehow made our beer lower quality or less genuine. In fact, the opposite was true. Our contracts were specifically written to allow us complete oversight and control over the brewing process. We brought in our own expensive noble hops, our own malt, our own yeast (propagated in Boston and shipped in refrigerated kegs), and our own brewmasters. At most contract breweries we used, we invested in new or retrofitted equipment designed to our own high standards so that they could make our product. I traveled to our contract breweries and tasted samples from every batch of our beer. Since then, I've continued to taste samples from every batch of beer we make.

Brewers who had gone up against us at the Great American Beer Festival also claimed we had gamed the system by showing up with scantily clad showgirls, what people termed "babes in bikinis." (Point of fact: These alleged showgirls were none other than Rhonda and Sally, and there wasn't a bikini in sight. I have the pictures to prove it. In 1986, Boulder Beer had the booth next to us, and they hired a model in a gold lamé jumpsuit to promote their golden blond ale. I believe that is how the rumor began.)

One of the most hurtful false accusations came from Brooklyn Brewery and its respected cofounder Steve Hindy, who triggered an investigation with the New York Division of Consumer Protection complaining that we were falsely asserting in a radio spot that Samuel Adams had "a head so thick you could float a quarter on it." He also complained that we hadn't really won the title "Best Beer in America." I didn't pay any attention at first, since our spot actually said you could float a *bottle cap* on it, which was true. (Try it yourself. It will float like a happy little boat.) And even more, I had the plaque we won from the Great American Beer Festival proclaiming that we were the "Best Beer in America"; Steve hadn't been at those festivals. I knew I was right, so I shrugged it off.

What I didn't understand was how the press works. I knew that journalists feed off of controversy. But I soon learned that even if allegations are false, the fact that they're false doesn't matter. The controversy *itself* is the news. Steve had been a successful journalist before getting into the beer business, so he understood this better than I did. *The Boston Globe* regarded the controversy as news and ran a story reporting that we had been accused of falsely advertising our accomplishments. Although the New York Division of Consumer Protection quickly dismissed the investigation, the damage to our reputation had already been done.

I was angry and hurt, but I learned several things from this and similar experiences over the years. First, if you're going to get out front and be successful, you're going to take some shots. Eddie Burke, the owner of Doyle's, a bar near our brewery, compared business to a dog sled race. "Jimmy," he told me, "you're the lead dog of this beer thing. You're out in front breaking new ground and pulling the sled. And when the other dogs look up and see you, what do they see? A big asshole! But remember, if you're not the lead dog, the scenery never changes. So keep pulling the sled and don't worry about the other dogs and what they see. And remember, you're all pulling the sled together." That last part was a good reminder.

I also learned to take a deep breath and embrace a longer view of things. When I am attacked, my initial instinct is to punch back, but this usually isn't the best response. It might feel good in the moment, but it can cause you to do things you'll regret later. Sometime after Brooklyn Brewery's investigation was dismissed, I learned that Steve had been involved with a tasting at a bar in New York where the bar had picked Brooklyn Lager as the top beer. Brooklyn Brewery then announced on their table tents that Brooklyn Lager had been picked as the "Best Beer in America" at the "Great American Beer Tasting," a claim that was confusingly similar and far less legitimate than the Best Beer in America award we'd won at the Great American Beer Festival. My lawyer told me I had a valid claim of false advertising. I decided to punch back, but my wife Cynthia (whom I had married in 1994 and was an entrepreneur herself) stopped me. "Are you going to be proud of that?" she asked. "I know you don't care now, but what about in five years? Will you look back and be proud of what you're doing?" She was right. I probably wouldn't. I was just angry. I had won (sort of) and I should just move forward. On many occasions since, I've asked myself if I was going to be proud of a given course of action, and I've stopped myself from doing something that would certainly have come back to haunt me.

Quite often, moving forward can have unforeseen benefits, giving you access to opportunities you can't anticipate in the moment. Years after the Great American Beer Tasting episode, Steve Hindy called me at home one night. A bunch of other craft brewers were forming a trade organization to represent craft brewers and he wanted me to be part of the group. The brewers were at a bar in Boston, and he asked me to come join them for a beer. The organization that emerged out of that meeting, the Brewers Association, has come to serve as an effective voice for America's small, independent brewers like Boston Beer and Brooklyn Brewery. I might not have become as involved so early on had I filed a false advertising claim against Steve and Brooklyn Brewery and continued the public battle. I also wouldn't have had a chance to work closely with Steve and to get to know him well. I'm glad I have: Over the years, I've found Steve to be a very decent and very honorable guy, even a courageous one (he had been a war correspondent and was taken hostage in the Middle East, and later had faced down a gunman trying to rob his business in Brooklyn). Not many craft brewers survived the early days, but Steve is one of the best of them. Today, while we remember our early battles, we share the common experience of helping build the craft beer industry. I think of John Adams and Thomas Jefferson, who patched up their differences to build an enjoyable friendship. I would not have had this pleasure had I continued what was ultimately a petty dispute.

In the heat of tensions between myself and Brooklyn Brewery, longtime head of the Beer Institute Henry King sent me a famous prayer that some attribute to Mother Teresa, called "Do It Anyway." King was an inspirational figure, a hero during World War II and afterward a devoted sponsor of impoverished children in Latin America. He and his wife adopted dozens of children and tirelessly raised money for orphanages, showing the difference that individuals with generous and magnanimous spirits can make. As I read the prayer, I understood why King had sent it. "If you are successful," one line read, "you will win some unfaithful friends and some genuine enemies. Succeed anyway." Mother Teresa's prayer concludes with the observation that, "In the final analysis, it is between you and God. It was never between you and them anyway."

Mother Teresa's prayer is great advice for anyone running a growing business. Her thoughts certainly helped me, enabling me to put things in perspective. None of the false accusations about us mattered. With time they would be forgotten. They were simply distractions. If I took the high road and continued to do what I believed in each and every day, all would turn out okay. So I did. And it has.

Stay strong. Keep focused on what really matters. Enjoy the scenery. Succeed anyway.

24

LAUNCH YOUR LONG SHOTS

I'VE TAKEN THE STORY of Boston Beer up to 1990, but let me back up a little bit to paint a fuller picture of what we were doing as a company and how the craft beer category was faring. By 1987, my little start-up was selling 24,000 barrels of beer a year (about $5 million worth), had expanded into eleven states and the District of Columbia, and had won Best Beer in America for three years in a row. I wanted to keep pushing us to do great things, so I started thinking about what other innovative beers I could brew. Our model was to create cool new beer ideas and to see if they would fly. In other words, it was to stay playful and pursue our simple passion for better beer.

We came out with our first seasonal beer, Double Bock, in 1988 amid mounting competition from other craft brews with standard pale ales and amber lagers. Nobody in the United States was making a great double bock, and I liked the challenge. Double bock is a spring beer, traditionally brewed by monks for Lent. The monks had to fast for the holiday. This was a tough rule, but like most tough rules, it had a loophole. They could still drink beer. So they made the strongest, most nourishing beer they could imagine, actually naming it Savior, or *Salvator* in Latin. Our first brews were pretty good, big and malty, and, like the German double bocks that set the standard, a little grainy from all the malt. I imagined a double bock that would be sweet, smooth, and creamy *without* the graininess. We tinkered with the brewing process, using only the first pressing of the grain in the mashing/lauter cycle, which yielded a cleaner, sweeter brew. This meant we had to go through two complete mash lauter cycles instead of one and use twice the malted barley (half a pound of malt, almost a loaf of bread, per bottle) for each brew as compared to a traditional double bock. The result was a much richer, creamier, and more delicious beer.

We initially intended Double Bock as a one-time thing, something fun that would push the envelope for American beer. Other brewers were doing one-offs too: Anchor had long made a unique Christmas Ale. Soon we began to introduce a variety of seasonal beers, including Octoberfest, Winter Lager (a spiced dark wheat bock as opposed to the winter ales other brewers were making), and Summer Ale.

As we kept brewing these occasional beers, I thought, *Hey, let's put them all together back to back and call it a "program"!* I believed drinkers would respond to that brewer-centric approach that said, "Here's a beer I love; maybe you will, too." Most small craft brewers were only making two or three beers and none had created a full program of four different seasonal beers rotating throughout the year. For the drinker and customer, a rotating array of special seasonals would be a whole new way of thinking about beer, one that captured the rhythm and customs of the seasons.

Creating a full seasonals program while maintaining the highest level of freshness was difficult. We needed to help bars manage transitions between seasonals so there wouldn't be a lot of stale beer in the market. That meant helping bars keep track of seasonals using one UPC barcode rather than one for each individual seasonal beer. Normally, each UPC barcode corresponds to a unique product, so we had to go before the trade group that controls the use of UPC barcodes to get it to approve a single code. And we had to create a new tap handle with a little flap on it so that bartenders could slide in a new label as the seasons changed. It sounds so minor, but nobody had ever done it before. It usually isn't enough to have a great idea. You also must attend to the details to make it work, and that takes time. Getting our seasonals program off the ground entailed a long, slow, incremental process of getting everything right. I saw once again that the execution of a good idea was the hard part.

Seasonal beers were just one of many new product launches during our first decade. In 1988, we came out with Samuel Adams Boston Ale and in 1989, Cranberry Lambic, an American version of a Belgian lambic ale. In 1992, we brewed 150 barrels of a Samuel Adams Cream Stout as a special St. Patrick's Day gift to Boston's large Irish-American population. By 1995, our year-round product line included a dark wheat lager, a wheat beer, a stock ale, and a cream stout in addition to our original Boston Lager.

Throughout this period, we were growing exponentially. In 1993, our sales grew 64 percent. President Bill Clinton served Samuel Adams at his inauguration and the president mentioned that Samuel Adams was his favorite beer. In 1994, sales again grew by 50 percent, giving us 700,000 barrels in annual production. In 1995, Ernst and Young named me "Entrepreneur of the Year." We were brewing our beer at our Boston brewery as well as at three regional breweries in the United States: the Pittsburgh Brewing Company, F.X. Matt Brewing in Utica, New York, and Blitz-Weinhard Brewing in Oregon. We brewed separately for European markets, using a licensee in Nagold, Germany. Overall, four full-time brewmasters supervised our quality.

Craft beer was on fire. Although still less than 2 percent of the overall market, it had become the darling of an industry that as a whole was posting flat sales year over year. Old-line breweries were now seeing up to 40 percent of revenues coming from the contract brewing of craft beers such as ours, and they were introducing their own craft beers, like Windy City Ale, Michael Shea's, and J.J. Wainwright. Small, independent breweries continued to open at a feverish pace (about one every other day in 1995), with an especially vibrant beer culture taking hold in the Pacific Northwest. "The microbrewery movement is going like hotcakes," observed Chicago brewer Steve Dinehart. "You keep thinking it is going to top off but it still hasn't, and it doesn't look like there is an end in sight yet."

While many of the new entrants brewed good beers with integrity, we saw an increasing number of gimmick brands named after house pets, wild animals, and colors. More worrisome were the actions of the larger breweries, which now were also getting into the mix. Budweiser introduced "microbrews" of their own—brands like Elk Mountain, American Originals, and Red Wolf. Miller bought up breweries like Shipyard and Celis, while Coors built on its Killian's brand, founded in the late 1980s. In addition, big brewers embraced many of the practices that I had pioneered and that had contributed to our success. Coors and Miller put out advertising that touted features like "deeper, richer color" and that emphasized the medals their beers had won at the Great American Beer Festival. Following our lead, the big breweries built direct sales forces of their own; in 1995, Miller hired fourteen salespeople in New York City alone. Seeing our success at the point-of-sale, big brewers also required that their distributors provide customers with the kind of acrylic customized table tents we'd pioneered.

Such developments prompted some observers to identify a bubble in the market. They forecasted an imminent shakeout, with many microbreweries failing or selling out to the major brewers. We at the Boston Beer Company were under no illusions as to our own vulnerability. Given how mammoth the big breweries were (Anheuser-Busch, the world's largest brewer, was nearly one hundred times our size), the playing field wasn't level; in a head-to-head battle, we were going to lose. To give ourselves a fighting chance, we knew we would have to learn some of the marketing tactics of the big breweries, something we did in 1996 when we unveiled our first television advertising. But our best chance at continuing the success we'd enjoyed to date would come from being agile, aggressive, and willing to expand our offerings so as to excite new beer drinkers.

We loved experimenting with beer, and we wanted to see how far we could go. Increasingly, I felt that the time was right to venture outside our brand again. Shelf space devoted to craft beer was exploding, and although we were 30 percent of the craft beer market, we were getting only 5 to 10 percent of the retail space. If there was room in stores for all kinds of cat and dog brands, perhaps we could expand our own reach by introducing new brands of our own. I was also conscious of the boundaries inherent in the Samuel Adams brand. Samuel Adams stood for classic styles of beer re-created in America with the very best ingredients. What else could we do?

Such thinking prompted us to launch Oregon Ale and Beer Company in Oregon. With our brewmaster Walter Scheurle living out in Portland, Oregon, and the strong relationship we enjoyed with Oregon's largest brewer, we thought we had a great opportunity to create our version of some of the West Coast beer styles. We wound up making an IPA, an ESB, and a raspberry wheat and nut brown ale using West Coast hops.

In 1996, we again branched out with a brand called Longshot that showcased America's very best home-brewing talent. A year earlier we had launched our World Homebrew Contest, a search for the world's best home brew in three categories: ales, lagers, and mixed styles. Finalists from among the 1,680 entrants were judged by a panel that included me, Dr. Owades, and noted British beer expert Michael Jackson. The three winning home-brew recipes were introduced to beer lovers across the country under the Longshot brand. Winning home brewers worked with our own brewmasters to guarantee that the beer we sold was faithful to their recipes.

That first year, Longshot produced an American Pale Ale, a Bavarian Black Lager, and a Hazelnut Brown Ale. We launched three more Longshot beers in 1997. Supporting talented home brewers kept us close to the small-scale home-brewing experience that was at our company's roots. No matter how successful you become as a start-up, it's critical to always remember the spirit that motivated you to get into the business in the first place. I had quenched my thirst for great beer and entrepreneurship by starting the Boston Beer Company. Now our company had the pleasure of helping a generation of inventive home brewers jump-start their own creative adventures. Ours wasn't the only thirst worth quenching.

THERE'S NO PRETENDING ABOUT QUALITY

INNOVATION FOR A GROWING company isn't just about new products. It's also about making existing products and internal processes better—something we also did during our first decade. In 1988, for instance, as we were expanding to new states and embarking on more distributor relationships, we introduced a couple of practices that greatly improved the quality of the beer we were getting to drinkers: freshness dating and beer buy-backs.

We had been attacking the imports for being stale, but freshness was an issue for small American brewers, too. Many drinkers don't realize that beer needs to be fresh to taste its best. It's not like wine; it's liquid bread. Most beer is only good in bottles or cans for four or five months before the hop character degrades, the slow oxidation that has been taking place all along starts to become noticeable, and the beer tastes stale. In the case of Samuel Adams Boston Lager, after four or five months the beer loses some of the top notes, the really nice hop aromatics. The analogy I like to use is the difference between hearing a musical performance live and hearing the same music on your iPhone. It's still the same Beethoven symphony or techno music being played, but the experience of listening on your iPhone lacks the richness and fullness you really want.

Breweries, whether large or small, imported or American, didn't talk much about freshness back then, and when they did, their talk didn't quite match their business practices. Unsold beer sat in distributors' warehouses for months, yet the breweries did little to replace the beer and take it out of circulation. They told wholesalers that freshness was *their* problem. Technically they were right; under the typical supplier contract, wholesalers had to maintain fresh beer and shoulder the whole cost of removing expired beer. But not wanting to piss off the wholesalers, and not greatly concerned with freshness, the breweries usually didn't enforce this part of their contract. Wholesalers in turn got good at playing a game I called "hide the beer," whereby they found an out-of-the-way retailer and sold them beer that was about to expire at a discount. I knew this because I had gone into a few retail stores in low-income neighborhoods and found large displays of expired Samuel Adams marked down, usually to half-price.

Let me emphasize: No outright deception was taking place when it came to freshness; rather, all of us were playing an elaborate and collective game of pretend. *Pretend* to stand for something. *Pretend* to care. *Pretend* you're giving drinkers fresh beer. You see this all the time in business, most often when you're dealing with big companies. Senior leaders might proclaim some lofty standard or principle, feeling good about "our values" and "taking a stand." Yet it's mostly talk—and everybody knows it. Management doesn't give the front-line people the resources they need to live up to it, so the front-line people have to figure out a way to do their jobs without making it too obvious that the principle is being violated. Nobody calls out the bullshit. The result is cynical disenchantment throughout the system. Employees see that bosses don't really care about the company's stated values, and they check out mentally and emotionally. They feel a little less positive about the work they do, or the organization, or the product. What customers usually see is a creeping mediocrity and compromise in the product or service being delivered.

In the case of our industry, drinkers were losing out because they were paying for a certain level of quality but weren't getting it. Drinkers and retailers couldn't determine whether the beer they were getting was fresh or two years old. Bottles came with a freshness dating system, but it was comprised of an indecipherable series of little notches on the side of the label that corresponded to a secret code. Each brewer had a different code that could only be deciphered with a cardboard "code card," so a drinker or retailer would have needed to carry twenty different cards with them to figure out if a bottle of beer was fresh. Obviously they weren't going to do that. The salesperson from the wholesaler could also turn a blind eye, since it was impractical for them as well to carry all these cards around and do the painstaking work of discovering a beer's date of production. *The supplier is making this too hard, so obviously they don't really care*, they would think, washing their hands of the responsibility. Stale beer in the marketplace was thus a fact of life, a by-product of the system that prevailed in the industry. No one player had established this system, so nobody was overtly guilty—but nobody had bothered to do anything about it, either.

All this represented a huge opportunity for us. We really cared about freshness, enough to deliver on that promise. So rather than play the industry's game, I did away with brewers' little secret by notching a freshness date right on the package that anybody could understand: "Enjoy before April 1988." No secret codes, just an expiration date in plain English. I then went further, offering our distributors amnesty programs. If they gave us back their expired beer, we would reimburse them. We eventually settled on a more permanent arrangement, taking any expired, unsold Sam Adams off their shelves and splitting the costs with distributors, no questions asked. This seemed fair: If a distributor had expired beer, it was probably half their fault for not rotating the inventory in their warehouse or at the retailer, and half our fault for encouraging quantity discounts that were too large, or selling a beer that didn't turn over quickly enough in their market to stay fresh.

This practice of buying back beer (which we continue to this day) was unprecedented in the industry. It's an added expense for us (in the early 1990s, we were destroying about $100,000 worth of beer a year, and it's now over $6 million a year), but it's absolutely worth it, as is the freshness dating—which maybe half the beers available for sale still don't do (Budweiser only started it in the mid-1990s). If you buy a pack of Sam Adams, you can see exactly where and when your beer was made, all the way down to the minute. As I told *Modern Brewery Age* in 1993, "losing customers is a lot more expensive than simply living up to the promise of quality implicit in being a microbrewery."

Sometimes, a strong visual is the best way to tell a story. In 1989 we invited bartenders to the brewery for a "beer-shucking" contest to see how fast they could open cases of expired beer. We then dumped all that beer into a giant tank, and I sat above it on a dunking platform. In exchange for a charitable donation, people threw balls at a bull's-eye. Lots of folks hit the mark, and I went into the beer over and over. We've repeated this event many times over the years. As I've often said, "I'd rather put people into stale beer than stale beer into people."

26

THE MOST EXPENSIVE EDUCATION YOU'LL EVER GET

AS A MATTER of principle, I believe that all failures are treasures to be valued; they let you see yourself in a new way, casting light on your existing erroneous assumptions and practices. In fact, the whole nature of my entrepreneurial journey had been one of learning by doing, and under that model, mistakes have been frequent. At my business school graduation, my father told me that my diploma from Harvard was *not* the most expensive education I would get. When I asked why, he said that if I continued in business, I'd start out by making thousand-dollar mistakes and work my way up to hundred-thousand-dollar mistakes. If I were really successful, I'd get to the point where I could make million-dollar mistakes. School was cheap.

He would be proven right during the late 1980s—and then some. In 1986, a year after our launch, the company was profitable enough for me to pay myself a $50,000 annual salary. I decided that the time was finally right for me to build my own brewery, as called for in my original business plan. I wanted my brewery to be in our current home: the historic Haffenreffer Brewery, the last operating brewery in Boston. The old brewhouse was still a total mess, with a fallen-in roof, no windows intact, pigeons roosting everywhere, and wires hanging loose. The drains at the loading dock had clogged up long ago, creating a small pond with soda cans and junk-food bags floating in it. My plan was to renovate the facility top to bottom and install classic copper equipment, restoring the brewery to its nineteenth-century greatness.

It was a romantic idea, but totally impracticable. The Haffenreffer Brewery was in a tight urban, residential area where it would be difficult to build, and we faced additional constraints because the site was a historic landmark. If we wanted to install tanks, for instance, it turned out we would have to take the roof off, mark every piece of it, and put it aside. Then we'd have to shore up the walls and gut the floors (since they couldn't support the weight of the tanks any longer). We'd have to build a steel superstructure inside the old building, hang the tanks from that superstructure, and replace the roof piece by piece exactly the way it had been. All to install a handful of tanks.

And we didn't, strictly speaking, even *need* a brewery of our own. Our contract brewing arrangement was serving us just fine and there were other high-quality breweries around the country that also had excess capacity.

I wasn't thinking rationally. I like to say that brewers have an edifice complex. Maybe entrepreneurs in general do. We feel we've accomplished something when we've built real, tangible objects that are ours. In the case of brewers, it's all about copper kettles and stainless-steel tanks. Stainless steel is like an aphrodisiac. You just want to embrace it, touch it, be with it, look at it. On top of that, breweries evoked childhood memories for me. As I told people, just being in a brewery reminded me of visiting my father at his brewing job. I remembered the light shining off the huge tanks; the rich, wonderful, warm smell of roasted grain; and the sense that something magical and mysterious was being created before my eyes. It just felt like home, and there would be nothing more fulfilling than to have a big, well-equipped brewery all to myself.

If I was guilty of anything in pursuing my own brewery, it was falling prey to a common pitfall of quick success: overconfidence. Throughout the late 1980s, I thought I could make all my dreams come true because everything I touched up to that point had succeeded. All the accolades ringing in my ears stoked my ego, which might not have been too dangerous if I had been dealing with parts of the business I knew well, like beer and brewing. Here, though, I was embarking on a major construction project, something I had never done before. Unfortunately, there was nobody around to bring me down to earth—no boss or board of directors. It was just me and my ambitious dreams.

We spent almost two years designing the new brewery and buying some of the equipment we'd need. In 1988, with the project looking like it was a go, I raised outside capital for the first time in the history of the company. Designers and contractors estimated we would need $8 million to get the brewery up and running, and I was able to raise $11 million from two sources: a tax-free Industrial Revenue bond that had an interest rate of 12 percent, and outside investors who chipped in several million dollars in exchange for 25 percent of the company.

I solicited formal bids from contractors to build the facility. The one smart thing I did was hold off on the actual construction until the bids were in and I knew the project's final cost. Many times, companies or governments start projects without knowing the final cost or schedule and they suffer from major overruns. Since I had taken the time to design the facility to the last valve and door knob, I had detailed specs that allowed firms to submit fixed-price, fixed-schedule bids. The bids came back and I nearly had a heart attack. Not $8 million, not $11 million—*$15 million*, almost twice the initial estimates. For the first time in two years, I was shaken out of my growth-fueled stupor and forced to look hard at the deal. Yes, I might be able to raise another $4 million, but if I went ahead with the brewery and it didn't work out, I might lose the company. Was it really necessary to take this risk?

I was tempted to go for it. After all, I'd read stories of bold entrepreneurs who'd had the courage to "bet the company," against others' advice, and who ultimately proved everyone wrong by succeeding. Wasn't I one of those? I wasn't. I asked myself whether the brewery was a "need to have" or a "nice to have," and I decided it was both. I always felt that we needed to have a brewery in Boston. We were, after all, the Boston Beer Company. But we didn't need to make *all* our beer in Boston; that wasn't going to make the beer better. So a small brewery was a "need to have" but a $15 million brewery was a "nice to have" and definitely not worth risking the company.

I also got good advice from an early investor, a former client from my BCG days who became a close friend, John Wing. John was starting to build the largest private power plant in the world, so he knew something about construction projects. He put the whole decision in perspective. When I explained the situation, John looked at me and gave me advice I still remember. "Jim, don't risk what you have," he told me, "to get what you don't need."

In September 1988, I pulled the plug. I had already bought most of the tanks and equipment for the brewhouse, to the tune of between $2 million and $3 million, and now I had to sell it at an almost total loss. I sadly remembered what my father had told me about million-dollar mistakes. It also occurred to me that thanks to one bad move, I had vaporized more money than I had ever made in my entire life to date. The company's balance sheet was in the red. In economic terms, I was a net negative. At the age of thirty-nine, despite years of planning and running a start-up company, I was no further ahead than I had been in Outward Bound. Still, I felt lucky. I had learned a valuable lesson and come to my senses, and the business had not been compromised too badly. With my edifice complex out of the way, our growth could start again.

I thought I could still build a small brewery, so I went back to the String Theory. I had hired Andy Bernadette, a brewmaster who was also an engineer, to take charge of the brewery project for me. I went back to him with a drastic change of plan. "Andy, forget the $15 million brewery. You have $200,000 and three months. Let's figure out what brewery we can build with that." It was a tall order; I would have understood if Andy quit on the spot. Fortunately, he didn't. I sweetened the assignment by doing what I could to give him a head start. A brewery in Albany, New York, called the Wm. S. Newman Brewing Co. was faltering, and the equipment (which was much smaller, simpler, and cheaper than what I had just sold) was available. I snapped it up for Andy. One day, while we were reviewing the initial drawings for the brewery to see how we could make it smaller and more affordable, I asked if there was anything else I could get him that might help.

"Yeah," Andy responded. "I need a Dave Grinnell."

"What's a Dave Grinnell?"

Andy grinned. "He's a brewer I worked with before. He can do anything in a brewery—electrical, plumbing, carpentry, rigging, welding, you name it."

"Well, go hire him."

"Easier said than done. I don't know where he is; I think he may be in New York City. It's a big place."

"Well, if you need him, find him. Figure out a way. Andy, I've seen you do some amazing things. Can you do one more?"

It turned out he could. Playing off the Madonna movie *Desperately Seeking Susan*, Andy took out an ad in the personals section of the *Village Voice*: "Desperately Seeking Brewer. Dave Grinnell, Call Andy." Sure enough, Dave was sitting on a park bench in lower Manhattan having a coffee and reading the *Voice* when he saw the ad. He called Andy.

I interviewed Dave at the Boston airport on my way to Munich for hop selection. We hired him, and two months later, in November

1988, our small brewery in Boston's old brewing neighborhood was up and running.

I'll never forget that first brew. Our machinery was pretty basic and old-school microbrewing; we were making beer the way it was made in Sam Adams's day. All we had for a lauter tub (the place where you separate the liquid wort from the spent grain) was a big round tank and handmade straining plates. A more advanced brewery would have had an automated rake stirring the liquid to prevent the grain from caking up, but we had to stir it by hand with white, food-grade shovels. It was backbreaking work. No, our brewery wasn't the Trump Tower of brewing, but I felt deep satisfaction because this 120-year-old abandoned brewery was once again filled with the distinctive, wonderful smell of malt and hops. There is nothing like the aroma you get when you first put the malt into the mash tub and start heating it. So much has changed with brewing over the centuries, but not that warm smell of steaming grain. It smelled the same in the monasteries where the brewers did their work a millennium and a half ago. Walking around smelling that smell, I could sense the spirits of brewers past hovering over us in the place. I hope they were pleased.

In 1989, about eight months after we began brewing, we opened a visitor's center in the brewery so that we could greet the "beer pilgrims" who came for brewery tours. Hundreds of neighbors, friends, and members of the media showed up to help us celebrate, including the governor of Massachusetts, Michael Dukakis. This old, run-down brewery in a struggling part of Boston was now suddenly alive with beer and people.

We have since expanded the Boston brewery many times. Most of the beer we brew here is packaged in kegs, and we maintain a small bottling line for our specialty beers. Dave Grinnell has grown with the company and is now the Boston Beer Company's VP of Brewing, responsible for all brewing operations. A framed copy of that newspaper ad from the *Village Voice* hangs in his office. Andy had been exactly right: a Dave Grinnell was exactly what our company needed.

Sometimes we succeed, sometimes we fail. And sometimes we succeed *because* we've failed. Whatever the case, we need to accept our failures and even learn to laugh about them, a lesson that was brought home to me during our grand opening. We had created a six-foot-high, three-dimensional piñata in the shape of a Sam Adams bottle, and Governor Dukakis, who had lost the 1988 presidential election to George H. W. Bush a few months earlier, was invited to take a whack at it with a baseball bat. Children were crowded around, waiting for toys and candy to fall out. Dukakis took a Green Monster swing. *Whack!* Nothing happened. He tried again. Still nothing. *Whack!* No, he didn't break it open. A little kid who was standing nearby uttered, "George Bush woulda had it open by now."

Maybe that kid was right. But at least Governor Dukakis was still out there, swinging that bat.

27

WE TAKE BEER SERIOUSLY,
BUT NOT OURSELVES

COLLEEN KEEGAN WILLIAMS was one of the greatest salespeople we've ever had. She was smart, determined, and full of energy—a force of nature. While working full time for us, she had had five kids in six years. Yes, you read that right. I'm told she only slept four hours a night, and I believe it.

After her fifth child was born, Colleen finally packed it in, leaving us with an endless number of funny Colleen stories. Once she pulled a practical joke on a prospective new employee. As part of the interview, he spent a day in the market with her. They were in a convenience store and he asked the manager if he could use the men's room. Colleen grabbed a Dixie cup and told him she wanted to do an impromptu drug test. He came back with the filled cup and Colleen couldn't stop laughing.

Another time we were at a company meeting in New Orleans, staying at a Holiday Inn on Bourbon Street that had small balconies. That night, with the streets teeming with people, Colleen and her colleague, Michele Burchfield, stood on one of those balconies and saw other people either mooning folks or throwing beads to the crowds below. Instinctively, they grabbed stacks of cardboard Samuel Adams coasters and started launching them, like little Frisbees, to the eager throng. Strings of beads don't build awareness for your beer—but flying coasters do.

Colleen was not alone. There was much merriment at that particular company meeting, held the week before the Super Bowl. Across the street from our hotel, a vacant lot was filled with Anheuser-Busch inflatables, dozens of ten-foot-high Bud bottles and cans. The bartender told me they had just taken advantage of an empty lot with an absentee owner and didn't get permission. Of course, whether or not this was actually the case, this sight bugged us. After midnight, one of our salespeople decided to stage a commando raid. She borrowed a knife from a bartender, and with the knife in her teeth she scaled an eight-foot-high fence. Within minutes she had made mincemeat of the inflatables. Then, she put the knife back between her teeth, climbed the fence again, and dropped back onto the sidewalk just as a police officer rounded the corner. He caught sight of the scene and looked at our pirate. She hid the knife and started to cry. "I can't believe somebody did that," she bawled. "I work for the brewery, and I spent so much time working on those!" The officer shook his head, "People can be animals sometimes," he said, and walked away.

At another company, a little crazy behavior might have gotten you fired. We tolerated it, maybe even relished it. It was part of our culture, what set us apart. As a young and growing company, our culture was about working hard and putting all of ourselves into everything we did so that we could come up with creative, intelligent solutions to problems. It was about having fun, not bowing automatically to external rules, and not taking ourselves too seriously. Work hard. Play hard.

When Rhonda and I left good jobs to start Boston Beer, each of us did so because working at our little start-up let us live our dreams and do what we loved. We got to drink delicious beer and hang out in bars and out of that came a whole new industry, even a movement. What could be better than that? Our passion and adaptability set us apart from the big breweries, whose employees tended to be more detached from their jobs and also more rule-bound. If one of our sharpest, most enthusiastic, most hardworking employees whipped coasters at people off a balcony in New Orleans, where's the harm? I know it doesn't sound like something you necessarily want your people doing; I didn't necessarily want it either. But it was way better than the alternative of playing it safe. And, after all, it *was* Bourbon Street in New Orleans in the early hours of the morning. It probably wasn't the most outrageous behavior in the Quarter that night, probably not even at that moment.

While working for BCG, I had seen large companies fail to live up to their potential because of internal politics, a disengaged workforce, unhealthy management practices, and other elements of a weak culture. I realized then that culture and people were *way* more vital to a company's success than the right strategy or achieving superior scale. If you engage people and inspire them to do their best, if you can create a work environment where people *want* to excel, then you can create products or services that will consistently outperform the competition.

As your company succeeds, make sure that you continue to nurture the culture that's making you successful in the first place. Even today, having fun remains one of our most important rules. As I tell our people, when my first two kids were born, we had a diaper service. They gave us thirty cloth diapers the first week. We left soiled diapers in a pail on our front porch, where they festered and fecundated in the summer heat until the weekly pickup. The next week, they dropped off the exact same number of fresh diapers as we had returned. If we gave them twenty-nine dirty diapers, we got back twenty-nine clean ones. In other words, it was somebody's job to pull the stinky diapers out of the pail and count them one by one. Not so much fun. I remind our people that we don't have *that* job. And I tell them that if they have a tough day, they should remind themselves that they're not counting dirty diapers.

Our job, by contrast, is to make people happy. It's fun by definition. If we're not having fun in *the beer business*, we're not doing our job right.

28

THE CEO FLIES COACH

AS AN OUTWARD BOUND instructor, I led groups as we grappled with unanticipated occurrences: sudden storms, extreme temperatures, injuries, trails that existed on the map but didn't exist in real life. We had to live by what we carried, and my job was to set the tone, establish the energy, and get people working together to meet challenges. I couldn't be tired, frightened, discouraged, or depressed because if I was, everyone else would be, too, and then we'd be screwed. The leader is never tired or depressed. Never.

Sometimes a macho guy would want to move faster than the rest of the group, showing off by reaching the day's campsite destination first. This was a pain in the ass because in Outward Bound the instructor had to keep the group together and that meant you moved at the speed of the slowest person. It was dangerous if your group was strung out with someone out of sight in front. You didn't get there until you *all* got there.

I needed to teach the macho guy a lesson. Let's say a guy like that got out in front and separated from the group. If he reached a fork and went down the wrong path, I would let him go. Then when our group was ahead on the right path, I had them rest and wait while I went back for the macho guy. When the two of us finally rejoined the group, the others—the allegedly "weaker" ones—would glare at the guy for adding an hour to the day. Because Mr. Macho was willing to put strength over team, he had slowed everyone down.

Reflecting on this lesson, I told novices that I wanted to teach them two basic things. "First," I said, "I'm going to teach you to be strong because you're going to need that. Second, I'm going to teach you that the reason to be strong is so that you can be kind."

It was true. Everyone on a trip needed to know how to carry their share of the load without feeling hopeless or getting exhausted and weighing everyone else down. And the strongest members needed to be willing to notice the slower people on the trail and take some of the weight out of their packs. Then the group would move faster. Unless stronger individuals on the team were willing to help the weaker, the group would never reach its potential. We either succeeded together or not at all.

Teamwork and the leadership that underpins it are also vital in business. As a company succeeds, it's easy for executives to develop egos and to forget about the perspectives and concerns of everyone else. Leaders get glorified and rewarded as if they were the primary reason for a company's success. Usually, they are not, and almost certainly they are not if they claim credit for the company's success. At Boston Beer Company, I soon realized that I couldn't really do much. Sure, I could sell my one or two new accounts a day, but that wasn't enough to help us reach even our modest goals. I needed help. I needed to be part of a team. All leaders owe their success to followers. If you forget that, you're no longer a leader. And sometimes even the leader is a follower.

It's important not just to mouth egolessness as a leader but to live by it. For instance, I've never wanted a fancy car. When I started Sam Adams I had a beat-up yellow Chrysler K-car station wagon—a Lee Iacocca special. Since then, I've driven a series of Hondas, and recently I moved up to a Ford Hybrid. It does everything well that a car should except for one thing: It doesn't impress people. And that's the point. Why would you want to impress people who are impressed by the car you bought? Those people are idiots by definition. Why bother to impress idiots? I also don't want everyone else to think that vanity and egotism are values our company encourages.

I've never been the highest-paid person at Boston Beer Company. I've done very well financially because the company has succeeded. I've always been fine with paying others more because it tells people that I recognize I'm not the most valuable person. Likewise, everyone at Boston Beer Company flies coach, including me. On those long trips to Munich, the upgrade from coach to first class is an extra $5,000. I can't make the math work—the average person at Boston Beer makes $55,000 a year. How can I justify paying over a month's salary for a first-class ticket? Is having me get a little more legroom and a better meal really more valuable to the company than what the average person contributes every month? I've never believed that.

Likewise, when I go into a market, I don't just meet with the marquee accounts. Instead, I ask our sales team to take me to meet with customers we're having trouble with, even if they're small. I learn more and can usually be more helpful talking to these customers. We have to work together to get the job done so the company as a whole benefits.

All of this might sound mundane, maybe even a little too high-minded, but every small thing that leaders do sets the tone and increases team members' commitment to the common cause. People are always sensitive to hypocrisy or compromises from managers, and the behavior of senior leaders is scrutinized, magnified, and commented on by everyone. Leadership is a privilege, but in the immortal words of Spider-Man, "With great power comes great responsibility"—the responsibility to be a good role model and to practice what you preach.

THE "FUCK YOU" RULE

ONE OF MY SCARIEST experiences at Outward Bound happened because I said nothing. We were going through a quarter mile of Class III whitewater, scary but not dangerous if done right. Normally one instructor went through the rapids first to check them out and wait at the bottom. The students observed and then followed one by one. If any of them flipped over, the instructor was there to help. This time, the director of our program, who was a very good boater, went down the rapids and then motioned for our assistant instructor, who wasn't so good, to lead our entire group of beginners down all at once instead of one by one. I was to go last to take care of anyone who capsized. When I say beginners, I mean that all the training these people had was a day on a lake learning the Eskimo roll, high and low braces, and a few paddling basics. I thought it was a bad idea, but I didn't say anything; I didn't want to contradict the director in front of the group. I was only an instructor, and I assumed the director knew what he was doing.

The water was rougher and the other assistant instructor less skilled than the director thought. The assistant went into the rapids, got out of position, and capsized halfway through. He couldn't roll back up because the water was too turbulent. When the students saw him flip over, they lost it, forgot what they had been taught, and capsized too—boom, boom, boom, boom. Within ten seconds, the entire patrol of eight people, plus the assistant instructor, had flipped over into the whitewater. Nine boats, nine paddles, nine bodies were spread all over in the rapids. These were just twenty-year-old kids, and they all could have been killed. Get pinned the wrong way against a rock with whitewater rushing at you, and it's over; you flail helplessly until you drown. I went into the rapids to get as many people as could hang onto my kayak.

Thank God, we managed to get everyone safely to shore and out of the water (though we lost a paddle). It was such a close call that I literally pissed in my wetsuit when it was over. I was wet, cold, tired, and furious. The assistant instructor quit right then, in the middle of the course, disgusted with the bad decision-making of the course director. I didn't blame the assistant instructor. I blamed myself because I didn't have the courage to take on my boss and say what needed to be said. This experience haunted me, and I resolved never to stay quiet again.

Many companies are plagued with disconnects between what managers and employees say they do and what they *actually* do. These disconnects persist because nobody steps up and speaks truth to those with more power. Chris Argyris, a business theorist I worked with at BCG, would talk about the left side of the page versus the right side of the page. The left side of the page was what people were thinking and feeling, while the right side was what was coming out of their mouths. The further apart the pages get, the more dysfunctional interactions within companies become, and the more company performance suffers. People know important things but feel afraid to talk about them with their managers.

IF YOU READ the cartoon *Dilbert*, a good part of the humor has to do with undiscussable subjects within companies. It goes like this: The organization is doing something stupid and the people at the bottom realize it, while the people at the top aren't close enough to reality to grasp the stupidity. Unfortunately, the people at the bottom have been taught not to speak up. If they try, they're told, "That's the way they want it" or "That's the way we do it." If they keep trying, they get sanctioned, branded a malcontent or not a team player, or even lose their jobs.

As time passes, everybody decides that the people responsible for the company's stupidity (or worse, a nameless "they") are idiots, even though nobody ever bothered to speak up about the idiocy. The stupidity then becomes undiscussable. And then within the organization, the fact that it's undiscussable itself becomes undiscussable. The organization ends up fully committed to doing things that most people in the organization know are ineffective or wasteful but that those same people pretend are not stupid and all keep doing. Meanwhile, observers on the outside laugh at these poor souls who are trapped in foolishness that they themselves realize is foolish. Companies do this kind of thing all the time. And the creator of *Dilbert*, Scott Adams, has made a career bringing it to light so we can laugh at stupid things we do ourselves and are powerless to stop.

When I started Boston Beer Company, I wanted to avoid ever having my company become a *Dilbert* cartoon. So, I instituted what has come to be known affectionately as the sacred Fuck You Rule. It's simple. At Boston Beer Company it's okay to say "Fuck you" to anybody in the company—including me—if that's how you really feel. But you can't *only* say "Fuck you." "Fuck you" is a purely emotive statement. It's like a grunt. Once you've let out your grunt, you also have to explain to the person why you said it and what the other person did to make you feel the special "Fuck you" feeling. You have to listen to the other side of the story, because there is always another side. Finally, there's no point in saying "Fuck you" to a person who is not capable of fixing the problem. You have to go to someone who can effect change, for only then do you stand a chance of collaborating on the solution.

The Fuck You Rule is basically just a restatement of the Bible's Golden Rule (albeit in decidedly nonbiblical terms). The Golden Rule says do unto others as you would have them do unto you. Many people apply this principle incorrectly, maybe because it's usually taught incorrectly. They think "do unto others" means be nice to people, be considerate of their feelings, don't upset them, don't cause stress and conflict. Let me ask you something. Do you want people to be polite and not upset you? Or would you rather have them tell you the truth about what they're thinking, even if it's disturbing? Of course you'd want the truth. If someone's unhappy, and you're responsible, you'd want to know what you've done so you can fix it. "Be honest"—that's what the Golden Rule requires. Say "Fuck you" when you need to say "Fuck you." It's better than being nice to avoid talking about the truth.

The Fuck You Rule has been invoked with me maybe half a dozen times that I remember, and I think I remember them all. On one occasion, one of our top salespeople, Lewis Goldstein, had opted to move out of sales and into brand development. I had worked the market with Lewis several times, and after a few months I could tell he wasn't happy. I asked around, but nobody could or would tell me what was wrong. I decided to do Lewis's performance review myself and try to get Lewis to say, "Fuck you, Jim." I didn't succeed at that, but I got close. When Lewis told me to "Lick my ass," I knew I was making progress. Then, as required by the Fuck You Rule, he told me why.

Lewis was pissed off because, as he saw it, I often disparaged marketing, dismissing it as the navel-gazing stepbrother of the company's real engine: the sales force. Brand development was marketing, not sales, so Lewis felt like he had been demoted. I was, in fact, pretty harsh on marketing; I was going around comparing it to masturbation. But I hadn't realized the full consequences of what I was saying because nobody had ever called me on it. Now that someone had, I had to do something about it. If my public denigration of marketing was bothering Lewis, chances are it was bothering others. I'm glad that Lewis colorfully told me that he worked hard and contributed and that I should appreciate the important work he and others in brand development were doing. That refreshing bit of candor helped make us a better company and me a better leader.

The mere knowledge that we can say "Fuck you" at Boston Beer has helped us avoid some of the layers of bullshit that pile up in organizations. Certainly, it has helped keep me accountable. Best of all, we've avoided a nightmare scenario akin to all those novice kayakers at Outward Bound tipping over. As of 2016, we still haven't flipped and drowned (though we have sometimes come close). And to ensure that we don't in the future, I personally make a point of teaching the Fuck You Rule to all new employees on their first day at orientation. I also make a point when I'm in the office of looking at the cartoons people have taped up in their offices. If I start seeing *Dilbert*, I'll know we have a problem.

30

ALWAYS RAISE THE AVERAGE

WHILE I'M REMINISCING about Outward Bound, here's one more memory. One of my best students was a fifty-four-year-old high school teacher. When I first learned that we'd have a fifty-four-year-old woman on patrol with us, I was skeptical she'd make it. It turned out she was so good she almost served as my assistant instructor. She was physically weaker than the others but able to deal with anything you threw at her. Why? Because she'd dealt with fifty-four years of challenges. Really hard things like a bad marriage, losing a job, having a student die of leukemia. A long day of steep trail was nothing compared to what she'd made it through. She took her time, but because she paced herself and took regular breaks, she was hardly ever the last person to arrive at camp.

As I've argued, bosses need to consider hiring people with *all* backgrounds, not just those with the standard credentials. Outward Bound grew out of the experience of the British merchant marines during World War II. German submarines were sinking British boats in the North Atlantic. Sailors would pile into lifeboats and brave the rough seas waiting to be rescued. A curious pattern emerged: The people who were surviving were not the young, healthy, fit sailors but the older, out-of-shape ones.

Like the schoolteacher I met, these grizzled seamen had already survived bad stuff in their lives and so were undaunted by spending a week or two bobbing around the North Atlantic. They knew from their personal experience that life can suck, that it can be truly horrible, but they also knew that complaining or feeling sorry for oneself wasn't going to do any good, and that people can rise to the demands of new challenges. Observing the hardiness of experienced seamen, the educator Kurt Hahn created Outward Bound as a structured way of taking younger sailors and putting them through scary experiences. The idea was to help them build inner fortitude, self-esteem, and an ability to confront their fears.

I saw seemingly unlikely people of every variety succeed in Outward Bound. Instructors whom I met had been medical doctors, helicopter pilots, grad school dropouts like me, and even a Matthew Arnold scholar. Their resumés didn't matter; you wanted them with you in the wilderness because you could count on them.

You'll remember that I applied this lesson when choosing Rhonda as my partner; she was a woman in an industry populated almost exclusively by men, and she lacked a bachelor's degree. She had a two-year degree in secretarial service from a community college, but my snobby Harvard background hadn't allowed me to recognize that as a "real" college degree. Afterward, as our company rapidly expanded, I continued to pass over people with beer industry experience, sales experience, and sometimes even college degrees in favor of other, seemingly less-qualified candidates. Of our first sixty salespeople, only five had worked in sales before. And by 1990, our sales team was about 50 percent female, which was totally unprecedented in the old-boy network of the beer business.

The sexist old guard in our industry observed all the women in our ranks and assumed we hired them for their sex appeal to sell our products. The truth was completely different. When God created capable, resourceful, talented, energetic individuals, She made half of them women. And as I began to hire salespeople, I found that women were generally stronger candidates precisely because they had been discriminated against. Mediocre men had been hired over talented women, leaving a greater pool of female candidates. Hiring as many women as we did men meant we got better people.

If I was paying less attention to traditional credentials, what criteria was I using in making hiring decisions? Well, first, I had a very simple and strict standard: Never hire someone unless they raise the average. The only way the company could improve and grow was if our people improved and grew. Training was one way to accomplish that, but we also had to hire better people. We waited to hire for a position until we found someone who would improve the average— someone who was *better* than the person or people currently doing the job. Our record, I think, was taking eighteen months to fill a salesperson's job. We could only afford to hire one person to cover the state of Arizona, and we needed it to be the right person. That person turned out to be a woman named Andrea Warner, who as of 2016 has been with us thirteen years and counting. Someone who raises the average is worth waiting for.

Besides enabling us to bring in the best new people, hiring to raise the average helped us by challenging our existing people to get better. It also made the job of recruiting more challenging. Finding the best people is always hard, but under the "raise the average" principle, every hire counts. Recognizing this, we give our recruiting team the time and tools required to find people who will truly make us better. We've done this from the very beginning; when we first hired a recruiter as our employee number twelve, her mission was to hire just six great people a year. If she found one great person for us every two months, she was doing a wonderful job.

With the principle of raising the average in mind, I relied on behavior to determine whether a candidate would in fact fit the bill. I took an intuitive and observational approach to hiring, noticing people whom I saw naturally behaving in a way consistent with our values and asking them if they would enjoy working for us. It was important, I thought, that anyone we hired be a unique personality and be passionate about his or her job, just as I was passionate about mine. But you couldn't discern personality or passion by interviewing someone. You needed to see them in action. Studies have validated this belief of mine, showing that job interviews are only marginally better than handwriting analysis in determining whether someone is right for a job (in other words, neither is very good). In large part, this is because many people are good at figuring out what the employer wants to hear.

If you're looking to hire for your company, venture into real-life settings to observe behavior. I tended to find people in the bars and restaurants where I would sell and interact with drinkers. A good example is Colleen Keegan Williams. I first met her in 1986 when she was working in a bar in D.C. called Rumors. I was doing one of my usual staff trainings. She was asking unusually intelligent questions and had a fun, lively demeanor. After the training finished, I approached her and started a conversation. She told me she had been a finance major at George Washington University, played basketball, and was looking for a "real" job. When I asked if she had ever thought about selling beer, her eyes brightened. "Selling beer? That's a job? I'd get paid to sell beer?" She had all the ingredients—passion, smarts, charisma. I had a sense that she would work out great for us—and she did. Not all of our nontraditional hires were as successful (note: poop on Jeannie's desk), but most of the time they improved our company's average level of competence and skill, catapulting us forward.

Today, we hire new salespeople through traditional human resources channels, but we still include "ride-alongs" as part of the interview process so we can observe behavior in the field. This process weeds out about 30 percent of the prospective hires who passed all the traditional interview tests. People think that selling beer sounds cool, but then they encounter the blood and guts of the business. They see the greasy back-ends of bars, not the shiny front. They learn about unglamorous tasks like building displays, going into coolers, and changing draft lines. And many decide this isn't exactly the superficial, all-day fun they had imagined.

We also use other tools to enhance the interview process, such as a short, standardized work-style profile test we started giving to prospective hires back in the 1990s. As we've learned, it helps to hire people who enjoy the specific tasks they will perform while serving in a given job. The profile test helps us determine what activities people enjoy doing, and hence whether they're likely to *love* working in their job with us.

We once interviewed a man named Hank for an accounting position. I looked at the results of the test, which measured prospective employees' need to be proactive and take initiative, their need for order and structure, their need for social interaction, and their tendency to perform tasks patiently. His test revealed that he liked to take the initiative and interact with people and that he had little patience or need for structure. That didn't seem to square with the job of an accountant. You don't want an accountant to take too much initiative or you'll get creative accounting. You don't want someone who's too social, because accountants mostly work by themselves. And especially, you want people who are patient and enjoy structure. Hank had the profile of a good, happy beer salesperson—someone who would raise the average. As an accountant, he'd be merely adequate and probably unhappy.

"Hank," I asked, "do you like being an accountant?"

He thought about it for a moment. "Nobody's ever asked me that before. Actually, I don't like it much. I really don't."

"Well, why do you do it?"

He shrugged. "My dad was a CPA, and he told me that if I got my CPA license I'd always have a good job and make a good living. And he was right. I've had good jobs and have made a good living."

Now I had an idea. "Hank, have you ever thought about selling beer?"

His face brightened. "Selling beer? Really? That would be a lot of fun. I'd love to sell beer."

We didn't hire him for the accountant's job. Instead, we offered him a job as a salesman. He was promoted twice and married another beer salesperson at Samuel Adams. Beer really does change lives.

This principle of only hiring people who are better than the ones we currently have means we don't make desperation hires to fill an open position. And the raise-the-average rule makes hiring decisions surprisingly easy. It's easy to visualize in your mind the average person in your sales force or on your brewery floor or even in senior management and it's easy for your intuition to evaluate whether a candidate is better than the average person. Your gut will tell you.

If you're used to traditional hiring, you might feel uncomfortable turning to intuition. Aren't we taking too big a risk by relying on our gut feelings about somebody rather than rationally assessing facts such as past experience or education? I would counter that we're fooling ourselves by *not* relying primarily on intuition. As recent neuroscience has shown, our brains don't work rationally. If you hook a functional MRI machine to a chess grandmaster, you find that the best of them are not rationally calculating their next moves; they're *imagining* what will happen, unconsciously bringing to bear the hundreds of thousands of moves they've already seen. They're arriving at a feeling that guides their actions. They are using the nonrational part of their brain. The quantitatively logical part of your brain is pretty paltry. Just try counting by prime numbers while you're multiplying other numbers by seventeen. Impossible. But reading emotions by looking at someone's facial expressions while you're navigating a crowded sidewalk is easy for your brain.

If you try to make important business decisions too logically—be they about hiring or anything else—you're just distracting yourself. You need to gather and evaluate a lot of the right facts about a candidate, but ultimately, with those facts in mind, apply raw judgment to make a hiring decision. You're better off proceeding imaginatively.

Can you picture a particular candidate succeeding in this job? Can you create a movie in your mind of this person succeeding more than other candidates? What images or feelings does each candidate arouse in you? Maybe that will help you get that exceptional talent that your competition doesn't see—talent that will raise the average. A middle-aged junior high school teacher working as a hiking instructor? A twenty-something waitress or a trained accountant becoming a fantastic beer salesperson?

Why the hell not?

31

MAKE YOUR PUBLIC OFFERING PUBLIC

IF YOUR ENTREPRENEURIAL VENTURE grows long enough and fast enough, chances are you'll eventually have to figure out what to do with the company. Should you sell it and cash in? Should you become a publicly traded company? Should you hold on to the company, keeping it within the family? The best answer depends on how much control over operations and strategy you wish to keep, how much financing you need, your company's potential for further growth, and an array of other factors. If you do go public, as we did, I urge you to consider an issue that hardly ever gets discussed: How to do an initial public offering so that the *right* people win.

The Boston Beer Company went public in 1995, eleven years after the company was founded. We had been planning our initial public offering (IPO) for a couple of years, not because we needed the capital, but because I felt it was time to return value to my limited partners. (For those of you not well-versed in finance, an IPO is a "liquidity event," during which owners of a company can eventually cash out by selling part or all of their ownership stake on the open market. In a public offering, a company sells shares to individuals and institutional investors like pension funds and mutual funds. Afterward, shares of the company can be bought, and sold, allowing original investors the option of selling some or all of their shares.)

On a number of occasions, I had been approached about selling the company, a move that would have gotten cash back to original investors like my father, Rhonda, Sally, my old drinking buddies, and others who had invested a few thousand dollars each, but that didn't appeal to them or to me. I didn't want to sell the company. If I didn't have Boston Beer Company to run, I knew I would just start another brewery and hope it would become a great company. Why do that? I already had a great company!

Still, it had been eleven years, and although the company had succeeded beyond anyone's dream, my investors hadn't seen any money. On paper, the value of their investment had multiplied hundreds of times, but my investors needed actual cash to do things like pay mortgages and send kids to college. In addition, the venture capital fund that had given me money for my ill-fated brewery attempt back in 1987 was itching for us to go public so they could get their money out. So 1995 looked like a good time for our IPO.

The whole process of going public was a fascinating and sobering experience. As I discovered, a "public offering" was not public at all. For attractive offerings (offerings in companies that seemed poised for long-term success), only large institutional investors got in the "public offering." Not the public. This was the investment banks' way of rewarding the large institutions for also buying their other, less-attractive offerings. The large investors purchased the newly listed company's shares at an "opening" price, held them for a fraction of a second, and then sold them on the market once the price had "bumped" up as expected. By the time average investors got in on the action, the shares were often overpriced and the chances that they would lose money were high. Some of the highest-profile initial public offerings in recent years were great for the largest investors, while average, individual investors lost money.

In our case, the investment banks wanted to underprice our initial shares so that the price would bump up by 15 percent over the course of the first day of public trading, with all that money going straight to the institutional investors who were their best customers. Why would I want to give money to big investors? What did they ever contribute to our success?

When we sat down to negotiate the offering, I said to the investment banks, "I want my drinkers to be able to buy shares at a discount. Maybe it's never been done before, but there has to be a way."

They were flabbergasted. They had never heard of such a thing. Reward the little guy? The little guy was supposed to get screwed!

I had a conversation with an executive at one large investment fund who was berating me for wanting to sell shares to him at a higher price than the little guys got. He thought this was ridiculous. I asked him, "Do you drink much beer?"

"No," he said, "I have a wine cellar."

"I think you've proved my point," I told him. "All these little guys—they're my drinkers, so they're important to me. Why should I care about you? You don't even drink beer."

Unable to oppose the idea of getting discounted shares to drinkers on philosophical grounds, the investment bankers came back with all kinds of reasons why my idea of cutting average investors into our stock offering wouldn't work. "It would be illegal," they told me. "In order to sell stock, you have to give everybody a prospectus. The price isn't finalized until the night before the opening, and we ship it out the night before to everyone who's going to buy in the morning. How could we possibly do that when we're dealing with tens of thousands of small investors?"

It became clear that none of the regulations in place were designed to let me do what I wanted; we would have to improvise a whole new process in order to do what a public offering was originally designed to do. I'm reminded of an article I read about Christo and Jeanne-Claude, the artists who created public art installations around the world, including one in New York's Central Park called *The Gates*. It was made up of thousands of orange fabric panels hanging from gates set up over sidewalks in the park. Imagine the regulatory hassles involved in pulling *that* one off. Christo and Jeanne-Claude mentioned that the creativity in their art had two elements: innovation in imagining and creating the physical objects that made up the actual art, and innovation in handling mundane things like political opposition, zoning permits, licensing, and the hiring of contractors. You need the same levels of creativity to handle both. Lots of things in life are like Christo and Jeanne-Claude projects, and our IPO was a prime example.

The bankers offered a compromise: Reserve a certain number of shares for small, local brokers like Edward Jones to sell. But that wasn't good enough for me either. Edward Jones may have had brokers in small offices around the country, but if we gave them the shares, they would just reward their best customers by offering them a chance to purchase them and make money. I wanted to reward our loyal drinkers.

Negotiations with the bankers became a form of improvisational theater, a roomful of bankers and their attorneys against me. As our conversations wore on, it became clear: I wasn't backing down. My gut told me there would be a way to do what I wanted. From the very inception of the Boston Beer Company, we had been an underdog brand willing to do things differently. It might have been convenient for us to compromise in order to do a deal and get the pile of money that comes to the original investors in a public offering, but I was dogged in wanting to find a better way. Ultimately, I knew what the bankers wanted—money—and I knew that they were not going to let discomfort with my unconventional idea stand in the way of their payday. They couldn't do this deal without me. Taking Boston Beer Company public would be lucrative for them and their customers even if we set aside a large percentage of shares to sell directly to drinkers.

In the end, I prevailed. With the help of legendary venture capitalist

PRESS RELEASE

THE BOSTON BEER COMPANY
BREWER OF SAMUEL ADAMS
TO OFFER COMMON STOCK

Boston, Mass. August 24,1995 - The Boston Beer Company announced that it has filed with the Securities and Exchange Commission a Registration Statement for a best efforts initial public offering of shares of Non-Voting Common Stock. In this offering, each investor will be permitted to purchase $495 worth of stock. The price per share has not yet been determined.

It is currently anticipated that the offering will commence in mid October and terminate on November 9, 1995.

The Boston Beer Company brews Samuel Adams Boston Lager® and other handcrafted beers and ales.

Copies of the prospectus relating to this offering may be obtained by calling 1-800-495-BREW(2739).

A registration statement relating to these securities has been filed with the Securities and Exchange Commission but has not yet become effective. These securities may not be sold nor may offers to buy be accepted prior to the time the registration statement becomes effective. This communication shall not constitute an offer to sell or the solicitation of an offer to buy nor shall there be any sale of these securities in any State in which such offer, solicitation or sale would be unlawful prior to registration or qualification under the securities laws of any state.

Bill Hambrecht, who understood what we wanted to do and worked hard to help, we put a carefully worded press release (to comply with federal securities law) inside our six-packs announcing the offering of public stock. Consumers would mail in the press release to get a copy of our prospectus. They could then decide whether or not they wanted to participate in the initial offering. If they did, they had to mail in funds to purchase stock during a designated time period. Any investor could purchase a block of thirty-three of our shares for $495 dollars, or $15 a share—which turned out to be a 25 percent discount from the $20 a share that institutional investors got. The drinkers would do *better* than the big guys. Pretty cool.

We reserved almost a million shares in our initial offering for these small purchases, about a quarter of our total offering. We picked that million figure out of thin air; not having done anything like this before, I estimated that thirty thousand drinkers would send in money. We couldn't set aside too much stock for drinkers to buy, because if they wound up not buying in, our initial offering would be a high-profile flop. Would everyday drinkers feel comfortable sending in money to buy stock in our company using a coupon on our six-packs? We just didn't know.

Putting the information in our six-packs and getting the Securities and Exchange Commission to approve it cost us extra money, but it was worth it. About 130,000 drinkers mailed in their checks for $495 each, amounting to $65 million. We returned $50 million of excess funds and sold the stock to the investors whose mail arrived first. The offering as a whole was a wild success. After our "road show" in which we presented our company to institutional investors, we received orders for *twenty times* as much stock as we had available. Our stock price rose that first day from $20 a share to $33. Everyone made money: the institutional investors, our drinkers, and the friends and family who had had enough confidence to invest in my idea of "better beer" back in 1984. Advocates for small investors applauded us, with one expert telling *The New York Times*, "We think it's a fantastic example of how I.P.O.s should be available to individual investors."

As of this writing, that $495 initial investment in Boston Beer Company would be worth about $5,500. A significant fraction of the original owners—many of them my drinkers—have held their stock for twenty years. Prominent companies such as Google and Morningstar have since experimented with structuring IPOs in ways that allow individual investors in on preferred pricing, not just the big Wall Street insiders. With the Internet and changes to securities law, it's easier than ever to make IPOs truly public.

In retrospect, going public was a rite of passage, a sign that we had finally become a real company with a real future. I had always felt a lingering fear in the back of my mind that the good times would soon end. On my bad days, feeding our incredible growth had felt less like fun and more like a terrible burden. Imagine in the basement of your house there are these savage, insane, ravenous beasts, and they'll run upstairs and devour you unless you throw them fifty pounds of raw meat every day. Every day, every month, every year, I had to somehow come up with those fifty pounds of meat, representing pieces of my life. With our initial public offering, it felt like I could take a deep breath because Wall Street was saying, "Jim, you've built something here. You'll be around for a while." Best of all, I achieved this sense of stability while still retaining control over the company, since under the terms of the IPO I had been allotted all the class B, voting shares.

What I'll most take away from the experience of going public, however, is less positive: a new awareness of the world of Wall Street, where money is the center of everything. I've long proclaimed that getting rich is life's big booby prize, a message that might sound disingenuous coming from someone like me who has had the good luck to become wealthy. But I really do believe it, and the whole IPO frenzy confirmed my thinking. Entrepreneurs have to keep grounded when dealing with financial people. Otherwise, they'll get eaten alive or lose their souls. Financial people are about making money; there's nothing wrong with that—it's their job. But entrepreneurs are not only about money. There's much more to starting and building a company.

Late on the day of the IPO, a banker from Goldman Sachs called to tell me that the stock had closed at $33. "Jim," he said, "you've done very well. You're now worth $220 million, can you believe it?"

"That's ridiculous," I told him. "It's ridiculous for one human being to have that much money."

"No, Jim," he said, "you worked for it."

"No, I didn't. I worked hard, but not hard enough to justify that kind of money."

We politely agreed to disagree. Hanging up with him, I left the office that Rhonda and I shared and headed for the lobby. It was about 8 P.M., and a security guard was on duty, a man whom I knew from seeing him many nights. He was reading a book, studying for a computer course he was taking. "Jean Francois," I said, "let me ask you a question. Is this your only job?"

"No," he replied. "I work forty hours here and forty hours at another job."

"Plus you're studying."

"That's right."

"How much do you make?"

"Six twenty-five an hour."

Here was a guy who worked eighty hours a week, who studied whenever he could, and who still cleared only $500 a week. And here I was with $220 million. He would have had to work almost ten thousand years to make that much. I had worked eleven years. That's what I most remember from the day we went public, the insanity of that.

32

LEARN TO TAKE A PUNCH

OUR INITIAL PUBLIC OFFERING would mark the beginning not of a new phase of growth but of nearly a decade of stagnant sales. The culprit in the broadest sense was changing American tastes in beer and the bursting of the craft beer bubble. But we were also hit by one of my worst nightmares: a deliberate, well-funded, scorched-earth, multimedia campaign directed at us and at craft brewing by the biggest brewery of them all, Anheuser-Busch (A-B).

The campaign began with no warning in late 1995, almost immediately after our IPO, and it unfolded over about a year. Its target was Sam Adams and its vehicle was contract brewing, a practice that had been part of our original business plan and that we'd been pursuing with great success. Other brewers like Harpoon had attacked us in the 1980s for not disclosing on our labels that we were contract brewed. They argued that this was somehow "inauthentic" and deceptive, that we were offering a lower-quality product than we claimed. The practice is widely accepted in craft brewing today and continues to provide many good beers. It is now called "co-brewing," "partner brewing," or "gypsy brewing." But back in the 1990s, it was innovative—and controversial.

That was wrong. At the time, I said if Julia Child arrived at my house with bags of groceries and made dinner in my kitchen using those groceries, whose meal is it, Julia's or mine? Clearly, it's Julia's meal as much as the beer we contract brewed was mine. As I've suggested, our quality was much *higher* because of contract brewing. We were using better brewing equipment than we could afford at the time, had strict oversight and control, used our own ingredients and brewmasters, and invested in equipment upgrades to meet our own high standards. I personally tasted a sample from every batch of beer—and continue to do so.

Harpoon and other brewers eventually saw the light. They stopped their attacks once they began contract brewing, too. But the initial grumbling about our contract brewing never went away. It sort of faded to the background—until Budweiser, under its chairman August Busch III, developed it as a convenient and seemingly high-minded way to destroy Samuel Adams in particular and craft brewing in general.

Why would A-B, the world's largest brewery, want to destroy us? We weren't a serious threat to their empire. We were one one-hundredth their size. They literally spilled more beer than we made. The beer industry research A-B did might have played a role. For years A-B market researchers asked drinkers, "When you think of a great American beer, which do you think of?" and drinkers used to respond, "Budweiser." Now drinkers were saying, "Samuel Adams," and August Busch had been quoted in the trade media saying how much that pissed him off. I did try to reach out to Busch to iron out any hard feelings he may have had, but he never returned my phone calls or answered my letters. Once he even crossed a room to avoid talking to me at an industry event. I chalked it up to the arrogance of beer royalty. Why should he deign to respond to an upstart like me?

From Busch's point of view, our success and my own aggressive style in the promotion of Samuel Adams may well have come across as presumptuous. I was quoted from time to time as saying some provocative things, such as, "Once you've had a Sam Adams, it's hard to consider Bud the king of beers." Busch seems to have thought that he *owned* the entire beer business and that Budweiser really was the best beer in America, and he wasn't going to stand for my suggestion that Samuel Adams might taste better than Budweiser. In 1997, a beer industry executive was quoted in *Advertising Age* as saying, "I can tell you that the whole micro thing drives August Busch III absolutely nuts. It infuriates him that these upstart companies are coming in and implying that his family's product is lousy." In retrospect, I was naïve to think that the world's most powerful brewery would not eventually use its enormous resources to attempt to crush me.

A-B's campaign kicked off with a petition to the federal government proposing that all brewers be required to disclose on their labels who was the legal owner of the physical brewery assets. The Oregon Brewers joined the petition, lending credibility to A-B's position. They might seem to have been a strange partner for A-B in its attacks on craft brewers, but they were miffed because we had launched Oregon Ale and Beer Company. The media relations effort behind the filing was followed by a story on St. Louis's NPR affiliate and then by an Associated Press wire story that carried A-B's message and ran in hundreds of newspapers, and finally in *The Wall Street Journal*. I began to understand that this was probably just the first major salvo in what would eventually be a multi-tiered marketing campaign from A-B.

The biggest blow of all fell on October 13, 1996, when *Dateline NBC* aired a very negative twelve-minute story about contract brewing. I agreed to participate because a producer had told us it was a story on craft brewing that might also touch on contract brewing. When I say negative, I mean they put me in a darkened room and shined a spotlight on my face from below so that on camera I looked pretty evil. When the camera focused on A-B's spokeswoman Francine Katz, she was sitting beside a sun-drenched window, her face rosy and wholesome. During their interviews of me, NBC's Chris

Hansen pulled the old journalists' trick of asking the same "hard" question over and over again. "Jim, aren't you deceiving people if you say you've brewed this beer?"

I had dealt with the media for more than a decade, but I was no match for a full-blown attack campaign.

Then it got worse. On October 15, the first business day after the *Dateline* show, A-B ran full-page ads in the two biggest newspapers in Massachusetts, *The Boston Globe* and *The Springfield-Union*, reinforcing the *Dateline* theme and restating the inaccurate message that Samuel Adams was misrepresenting itself to the public; that our beer was the same or comparable to low-priced brands like Schlitz, Schaefer, and Genesee; and that our contract brewers were not using our recipes, ingredients, or processes when brewing our beer. A week later, radio stations in major markets nationwide ran A-B radio spots attacking Samuel Adams and me personally for contract brewing. In the spots, a historical Samuel Adams figure was heard coming to my house on Halloween as a trick-or-treater and saying something like: "Time to stop tricking beer drinkers, Jim. Treat them to the truth."

As A-B delivered hit after hit against us and other craft brewers, I wasn't sure how to respond. I wanted to hit back hard. Looking at A-B's own label, I knew we could attack them for such patently false claims as, "We know of no other beer that is as costly to brew and age." But I wasn't sure an aggressive reaction was in my own best interests. So far A-B had merely made life very hard for us, but if they really wanted to, they could put us out of business. I didn't want to risk antagonizing the eight-hundred-pound gorilla more than I already had.

Others around me agreed. John Wing asked me if I thought I could survive if I let them keep punching me without responding. I told him I thought I could. "Well," he said, "you might have to let them keep punching you. They'll stop eventually." John was no pacifist; he had gone to West Point and fought in Vietnam and other places and had the scars and medals to show for it. And he was my best friend. So his words carried weight with me.

I also called up Pete Coors, CEO of Coors Brewing, for advice. I had met him a couple of times and knew him as a genuinely nice guy. His advice to me was likewise to stay cool and take my licks. "Jim, what I've learned is that if you punch August in the nose, he'll break every bone in your body."

When I told our longtime lawyer I was considering suing A-B, he puzzled me at first by asking if I played polo. "What do you mean about polo?" I asked.

He repeated the question, "Do you play polo?"

"Of course not. I can't afford to play polo."

"Then you can't afford to sue Anheuser-Busch. You want to spend five million bucks and five years? Even if you win, no one will remember this in five years."

One beer veteran I called who had fallen out with A-B suggested that my personal safety might be at risk. "It wouldn't take very much for A-B to get someone to beat the crap out of you. A few words to one of their Teamster buddies might be enough." He told me that, after he'd left A-B, he made a practice of checking his luggage before going through airport security just to make sure nobody had planted illegal drugs in it. He advised that I not park my car in a dark place where a beating might occur unnoticed. At first I thought he was paranoid, but then I decided maybe he wasn't—he had been on the inside, so he knew A-B and its capabilities. I started parking under a big streetlight. It seemed crazy, and I had no idea if these allegations were true, but this was a new world.

As painful as it was, I did not try to punch back against A-B. My goal was to survive the war, not win it. What we did was create a response ad that essentially said, "We're flattered you guys think so much of Samuel Adams and don't worry, we'll keep making it so that you guys have our Sam Adams standard to aspire to."

We filed a complaint with the Better Business Bureau's National

Advertising Division (NAD) alleging that A-B's attack ads against us were false and misleading. Our complaint was a four-page letter; A-B's response through its big law firm, Skadden Arps, weighed two pounds and took up eight hundred pages—more of their efforts to kill a mosquito with a sledgehammer. After a five-month investigation, the Better Business Bureau found that A-B's claims *were* false and misleading. According to the Better Business Bureau, A-B's advertising had misled consumers about the quality of our beer and had falsely claimed that Boston Beer Company did not control the recipes, ingredients, and brewing processes used to brew Samuel Adams. They also found that A-B had made false accusations about me personally. As part of the Better Business Bureau's final order, A-B agreed to discontinue its ads.

We won on all counts, but it was a Pyrrhic victory. A slowdown in the craft category had probably been inevitable, but because of A-B's actions, the expansion of craft beer and our own success came screeching to a halt. Before the *Dateline* piece, craft beer's sales had been growing 25 percent. Within a month after the piece, sales growth for the entire craft industry dropped to nearly zero. Our own stock price had fallen to $11.75, less than half of what it had been a year earlier, and *The New York Times* wrote of "the sad fall of an IPO open to all." By 2000, some three hundred breweries and brewpubs had closed and the four largest craft brewers had experienced sales declines, leading some observers to dismiss craft beer as a fad that had seen its day. Our stock bottomed out again at about $6 per share; we wouldn't see double-digit growth until 2005.

Yet we had survived, and in my eyes that was winning. During the American Revolution, all the colonials had to do was hang together and remain committed, and eventually they won. After all, the British couldn't garrison troops throughout the entire country. And because the revolutionary cause was real, because it had taken hold at the grassroots level, the colonialists *would* hang together. A similar thing applied to us. We had been damaged, but there was something real and fundamental about the craft beer movement, so we had made it through. We had won. I took comfort in knowing who we were and what we were about. Nobody could take that away from us, not even A-B with all its billions.

If your company is growing and successful, eventually you'll find yourself in the crosshairs of some big company. You may not be able to win the battle, but if you survive with your forces intact, you can win the war. Don't make the mistake of fighting a battle you can't win, even if you're right. Try to focus on the good things, all the people who *do* support you. During the war with A-B, I was encouraged by the loyalty shown to us and me personally. Despite the public attacks and misleading advertising directed against us, some two-thirds of our initial thirty thousand small investors still held our shares a year later. Our distributors stayed with us, and some of our customers in the Boston area went so far as to banish A-B products from their shelves as a show of support to us. Many of our peers in the craft brewing community came to our defense, publicly speaking out on our behalf. And our team inside the company rallied together.

An especially heartwarming gesture of support came from our suppliers overseas. One of the rumored measures A-B took behind the scenes to hurt us was to try to buy up the global supply of the rare Hallertau noble hops we needed to brew Samuel Adams Boston Lager. At the time, only some five hundred acres of these hops existed anywhere in the world. If A-B had succeeded in buying them, we would have been severely damaged; we would have somehow had to find other farmers to grow them for us, or at worst, substantially alter our recipe. Fortunately, they didn't succeed and that was because of the loyalty of the hop dealer we used, Peter Barth. Peter and his family had no love for A-B. A decade or so earlier, A-B had sued the Barths for price fixing when they didn't like the price of their hops. The Barths fought for a while, only giving up when the litigation costs threatened to bankrupt their family company. A-B made the Barths hand over their largest hop farm in exchange for dropping the litigation. This time, when A-B tried to induce him to sell them the hops I needed, they refused.

Peter's family had been in the hops business since 1792, and there's a good likelihood that my great-great-grandfather bought hops from his family. I had worked with Peter since our founding and the two of us had been through some interesting times. In 1994, some of the German farmers who supplied us with noble hops were seeing their plants fall prey to viruses. Noble hops had never been genetically modified for disease resistance or high yields, and Peter had wanted to do away with them and have me buy cheaper (and in my view, lower-quality) varieties of hops. Every other brewer, including A-B, had given up on these noble hops. "You're the last major purchaser," Peter said. "You'll have to find a replacement, too, because all the experts agree, they're just too hard to grow."

I respected the German farmers and agronomists who were the experts, but I wasn't about to take their pronouncement at face value. I'd seen some farmers do very well growing noble hops, and I couldn't bear to see this principal heirloom hop of Germany's brewing tradition go extinct. English hop growers were successfully growing similarly vulnerable heirloom hops by practicing basic hygiene, such as washing tractor tires and boots, so that the plant disease wouldn't spread from field to field. Working with Peter, we sent agronomists to teach farmers these methods, helping to save the Hallertau Mittelfrüh hop from extinction. In the German beer industry, Boston Beer Company became known as the American company that saved the German heirloom hop. Years later, I would become one of only two Americans ever named Chevalier of the Order of the Hop. In the short term, Peter's respect for me prompted him and individual farmers in Germany to rebuff A-B when they wanted to buy up at a premium price the very noble hops that they had given up on. Their willingness to stand by me affirmed my longstanding belief that business really is all about relationships. Today, our relationship with Barth's company continues. There are about fifteen hundred acres of

Hallertau Mittelfrüh under cultivation, and I'm happy to say that we still purchase about 70 percent of them.

I sometimes reflect on the legacy of my unwanted, yearlong battle with the world's most powerful brewery and its strong-willed ruler. While they were focused on stopping Sam Adams, a bunch of very smart Brazilians were pursuing an international acquisition strategy that would catapult them from owning a modest brewery in a developing country to eventually taking over Anheuser-Busch in 2008 and kicking out the entire Busch family. August Busch, once the king of American brewing, was forced into retirement on the family farm. And I'm still here.

PART IV

MATURATION

(1996—MID-2006)

When the fermentation is finished, you might be tempted to take a sip. Not so fast; the beer still isn't ready. It needs to sit for a period of time—from a few days to a few months—and be kept cool. This "conditioning" phase allows for the deep, rich flavors to develop. Patience is a virtue in brewing, and in business, too. If you stay in the game and give your business time to mature, you'll find that the reward is far beyond what you ever anticipated.

GROW WHEN YOU'RE
NOT GROWING

FOR THE FIRST twelve years of Boston Beer, growth had averaged over 40 percent. Then, in one month, October 1996 to be exact, the growth stopped, and the long period of stagnation in our business began. You might think that this would have been tough to adapt to, but actually, it wasn't that bad. After all, we were still the same great people making the same great beer. Just because our growth stopped, we didn't get suddenly stupid. I wanted us to keep our heads up and continue to feel like winners. So I dramatically adjusted our expectations. Whereas 50 percent growth might have been considered a win before, now we would celebrate 1 percent or 2 percent growth. In fact, we could feel *better* about moving up 1 percent now than 50 percent before, since given the market conditions we faced, that 1 percent uptick had been even harder to achieve. I told everyone this at our annual all-company meeting so no one would feel disappointed that 50 percent growth had fallen to zero.

That's not to say we would sit back and simply do business as usual. We had succeeded since 1985 with a basic formula: make great beer, hire great salespeople, and support our efforts with effective promotion and education. Since expanding distribution was no longer a magic bullet, and there was no rising tide to lift all craft brewers, we would have to work harder just to maintain our position. Some wholesalers or retailers had moved on, focusing again on imported beers, so we needed to find new ways to get their attention. We would brew great beer and work our tails off to sell it, just as we always had, but we would have to do it more efficiently, better, and smarter.

When once-successful companies lose their magic, leadership often makes the mistake of trying to revamp everything overnight, bringing in a new CEO, new strategies, and new values from outside. As a BCG consultant, I used to see this "doom loop" taking hold. You had a good manager running a business with a business model that wasn't working any longer. Senior management started ramping up the pressure, usually without giving lower-level managers the resources or insights to fix the underlying problem. Once lower-level managers were in this position, they were screwed. Their bosses enforced a sense of urgency, demanding weekly or monthly reports about what managers were doing to fix the problems. This led managers to grab at short-term fixes, usually some form of cost cutting or layoffs to buy themselves time to understand and address the underlying problems. But managers never had enough time to do the work to get the business on the right track long term. Eventually, even great managers lost their jobs.

During the 1980s, when American industry was flagging and Japanese manufacturing was hot, people kept saying we had to be more like the Japanese. A book came out in 1990 by James Fallows called *More Like Us*. I knew him as a first-rate journalist and I read it. Fallows said we didn't need to be more like the Japanese, but that we needed to be more American. Our success would come from our own culture and values. And the 1990s proved him right. I thought a similar lesson applied to Boston Beer. The solution for us was to stay true to our values. They had gotten us to the point where the world's largest brewer wanted to take us out, and those values would get us to our desired future. We didn't need to be more like anybody. We just needed to be more like our best selves.

During the late 1990s and early 2000s, I traveled more than ever in order to keep our local sales forces motivated and excited. I somehow felt I could pull the company back into growth simply by force of effort and will. I visited thousands of bars and stores every year, maybe twenty thousand sales calls over the course of a decade. Meanwhile, we pushed the bar higher on quality and effectiveness. In my market visits around the United States, I noticed that when I ordered a Sam Adams on draft, it didn't meet my standards 10 to 15 percent of the time. So we trained our salespeople to do the same taste evaluation I did. To help bars improve how they cleaned the draft lines or handled our product, we performed tens of thousands of draft quality audits (ten thousand in 2001 alone). Five years later, our pass rate was 98 percent, the highest in the beer industry.

As far as retail stores were concerned, we introduced a simple program called "Sam to Standards" to help us determine if we were doing a good job getting visibility at a given location. We were the number-one craft beer, and we were determined to have more shelf space and better shelf space than any other craft beer. Our sales team went in to see whether we had more shelf space at eye level (the best possible location) than other craft beers, and also more "facings" (more units spanning the shelf) than any other craft beer. If we met these two criteria for a retail location, that was "Sam to Standards." Very simple. It sounds trivial, but we had never had a formal program before for determining if we were doing a good job in a store. Now we did, and it helped us compete.

We applied the String Theory, cutting waste consistently during the late 1990s and early 2000s and improving our profitability by tightening many areas of our operations. We figured out that on about 80 percent of our trucks we could fit twenty-seven pallets of beer instead of twenty-six. That one little change saved us four cents on a case of beer. Doesn't sound like a lot until you consider that we were shipping 16 million cases every year. We're talking hundreds of thousands of dollars of savings from one adjustment. In another instance, we saved $200,000 a year by using excess space on our trucks to ship our coasters to distributors from our breweries rather than from our warehouses. Once we loaded a truck with as much beer as we could fit, we still had some excess space, not enough for a whole pallet of beer, but space. That meant we could basically ship coasters for free. In yet another instance, we increased the number of visits our salespeople made in a day by using "street sheets" to plan their movements more efficiently. This system plotted a salesperson's daily calls geographically. It saved both time and energy.

We also worked to develop entirely new sets of skills within our organization. We had been contract brewing at the historic Hudepohl-Schoenling brewery, located in my hometown of Cincinnati. Like many contract brewers, Hudepohl-Schoenling was on its last legs by the mid-1990s. The revenue it received renting its excess capacity to us wasn't enough to make up for the poor performance of its own beer brands. Eager to retain stability in our production, we had been exploring a purchase well before the A-B controversy cast contract brewing in such a harsh light. In 1996 we signed an option to buy the brewery, and in 1997 the deal finally closed.

I'll never forget my father's reaction when I took him through the brewery right after we bought it. Dad was familiar with it; he had worked at Hudepohl decades earlier as a young apprentice brewmaster. All the same equipment was still there. As we went from area to area, he regaled me with stories about this or that piece of equipment. At one point, he stopped and shook his head. "Jim, we *own* this place?"

"Yes, Dad, we do. I bought it!"

I felt immensely grateful, like a son who had bought the mansion where his father had worked as a butler. For the first time, we would own a significant portion of our production capacity, though we would continue to contract brew the rest. We would also own one of the last of the small-batch dedicated breweries with employees who took pride in their work. Yet we faced some challenges. Founded in 1885, Hudepohl-Schoenling was dilapidated, located in a dicey neighborhood, and known as a strong union shop. The workers sometimes struggled to maintain the high quality standards we had for Samuel Adams, and the brewery needed equipment upgrades. We had no experience taking care of a large physical plant and managing Teamsters. We would have a lot to learn if we were to turn this historic, old-school brewery into a modern, highly productive craft brewery.

A typical buy-out company might have shut Hudepohl-Schoenling, let go of all the union workers, and hired new, nonunion workers before reopening. We weren't about to do that. Having worked during college as a low-level employee in factories, I'd learned that there are good unions and bad unions, just like there are good bosses and bad bosses. Most unions were good, I thought, and most employee problems were, in fact, caused by bad managers. As I observed, the workers in this brewery were well-meaning, hardworking people. They wanted to come in each day and make something they were proud of. We could engage with that attitude and build on it.

But we couldn't just waltz in and make Hudepohl-Schoenling like the rest of Boston Beer. We had to accept that the brewery's employees had their own culture, even though I believed they would have been excited about spending all of their time brewing a high-quality beer brand like Samuel Adams. I mean, Hudepohl-Schoenling's people wanted to make quality products—who doesn't? I learned that many of these employees were craftsmen who did things with their hands in their spare time, working on their motorcycles or handyman projects, making music, doing carpentry, and cooking (I learned to cook raccoon from one of them). They were eager to create something meaningful and worthwhile, so I knew that when they were focused on making our beer exclusively, they would feel proud of what they were brewing.

Our goal was to develop a version of the Boston Beer culture, one that met both our expectations and those of the brewery's hundred-person workforce. The key to this was to upgrade the brewery, showing Hudepohl-Schoenling workers that we cared about them and their work. To that end, the first thing we focused on wasn't productivity or even quality. It was safety. The best way to increase productivity is not to lower costs directly, as many people think, but to start with improving safety. When people are operating in a safe way, they're usually operating more confidently and carefully, which means they're operating in a way that will improve quality and reduce waste. Put money into safety, and you ultimately get a better-performing plant all around.

Investing in safety also improves morale. When we took over Hudepohl-Schoenling, Jeff White, a longtime Boston Beer employee who understood our operations and our culture, made it clear to workers that our priorities were safety, quality, and efficiency—in that order. "You come in here every day with your body parts intact," Jeff told them. "It's our responsibility to send you home to your loved ones with those same body parts. If we don't do that, we've failed you." We followed up by behaving in ways that showed we meant business. Our first hire was a safety supervisor, which the plant hadn't had before. We took care of obvious safety hazards, like machinery without proper guardrails, exposed electrical wires, or slippery steps, and took precautions like painting lines on the floor to mark where the forklifts operate (forklift trucks are the most dangerous thing in a brewery). We enforced rules like wearing safety glasses and hardhats. And we looked for talent in union ranks, soon promoting a union member to supervise implementation of the new policies.

We received a few complaints about the new rules, but overall morale soared. Hudepohl-Schoenling employees saw that we were anything but "corporate." We valued them, and it didn't matter whether they were union or management. Our safety lectures weren't just talk; we were spending real money to keep them safe. We were also pouring money into upgrading the equipment—replacing old brew kettles with new ones, performing preventive maintenance so, for example, the bottling lines wouldn't break down. We were there to stay, and we were providing the infrastructure necessary to expand our authentic, respectful brewing of a world-class beer. From the perspective of the employees, this made us the "good" guys.

Our safety record at Hudepohl-Schoenling has improved steadily over the years. Many people might think accidents are inevitable at a brewery, with hazards such as moving parts, breaking glass, steam, moving trucks, and objects susceptible to falling. Yet we now routinely go hundreds of days without a *single* accident. And happily, our productivity improvements have been dramatic. In 1997, the facility's one hundred workers made about 200,000 barrels of beer each year. In 2003, those same one hundred people were making *600,000* barrels—three times as many barrels per person. I couldn't have been prouder of them. They are my hometown heroes. And they were brewing those 600,000 with much of the same basic equipment as we had before, no fancy computers or automation. Owning a brewery was an exciting new advantage we had acquired, one that would serve us well when growth picked up once again.

To make acquisitions such as this and implement operational improvements, we brought in more talent throughout the organization. In 1994, well before the A-B debacle, we started looking for a manager of operations. The executive we hired, Martin Roper, turned out to be my most important hire, along with Rhonda. He had been a friend and classmate of my wife's and had finished first in their class of eight hundred hot-shots at Harvard Business School, had a master's in engineering, and had worked at BCG. As skeptical as I was of such traditional credentials, I came to admire Martin greatly; he seemed good-hearted, fair, really interested in people, and not greedy. Although he had received offers from investment banks and consulting firms, he had turned them down in order to run a factory in the rural Midwest. He had an obvious passion for making things, and for making them better than anyone else. With his rigor, discipline, and analytic ability, he would round out the passion and skills Rhonda brought to our sales operations. I was excited about bringing him on board.

My wife Cynthia helped us seal the deal with Martin during negotiations. "You're living in the middle of nowhere," she said to him. "Do you have a prayer of finding the future Mrs. Roper there?"

"Well, not really."

"You're not even getting laid, are you?"

He didn't respond, but we could tell the answer.

"I have a lot of single women friends in Boston. They're educated, intelligent, have good careers, are your age, and are looking for husbands. If you take this job, we'll find you Mrs. Roper."

And she did. Sometime later, we attended a friend's wedding with Martin, and Cynthia pointed out a woman in a red dress named Susan. Martin changed the name cards so that he was sitting next to her. Today, Susan and Martin live outside Boston and have three beautiful boys.

Martin proved himself to be a world-class manager and grew within the company, so in 1997 we made him our chief operating officer, with Rhonda continuing as founding partner and executive vice-president of sales. I was technically chairman and CEO, although my business cards read "Founder and Brewer," the same title I had in 1984 and the same title on my cards today.

At around this time, our leadership and our internal structures really started to grow up. I couldn't be Peter Pan anymore and we had to leave Neverland. We added a seasoned and tough business professional to our board who wasn't too impressed with how we'd been running our business; the phrase "amateur hour" got thrown around a lot. For the first time in our history, we did serious financial planning, creating budgets for our different departments and carefully studying potential expenditures. We systematized our human resources function, improving our procedures for performance evaluations, people development, and the like. We enhanced our training programs, building the skills of our workforce, which in 1997 numbered about three hundred. We had always been proud of our people; now we were empowering them in important new ways.

More professionalism brought a shift in how power worked inside Boston Beer Company. Until the late 1990s, everything had gone through me. I delegated tasks to others, but I made all the big decisions. I was happy now to see managers empowered *throughout* the organization; it meant I had to start listening to others rather than letting my vision drive everything. I felt comfortable with that because I believed in the culture we had built. Also, I realized that the organization was more eager for dispersed authority than I'd thought. We had a lot of great people who had grown up with us; it was time for them to take control and field true responsibility in their respective areas.

Developing internally as an organization is vital if a company is to pass from the start-up phase to maturity and stability. *Star Wars* offers a helpful analogy here. If the A-B episode had been like *The Empire Strikes Back*, we were now learning, regrouping, and strengthening ourselves much like Luke Skywalker and his band of rebels did after suffering setbacks at the hands of the Empire. No, we weren't hanging out in the swamp with Yoda, flicking around light sabers, but we were mustering our forces, preparing to get out there and do battle with the giants once again.

To my chagrin, not everyone was a *Star Wars* fan. In 1998 or 1999, during the height of the Internet boom and when we were in the depths of our doldrums, an investment manager from the West Coast came to Boston to pay me a visit. He insisted that I go to Logan airport to meet him. We were in an airport lounge when he said, "Jim, are you going to sell the company?"

I took a sip of my beer. "I have no current intention of selling the company."

"That's a problem for me. The way your business is going, there's no way I can make a 300 percent return next year on the million shares we hold."

"That's right," I told him, "you won't make that."

"But I can put my money into these Internet companies and get 300 percent in a year." He took a sip of his wine. "Okay, let me put it to you this way. If you don't sell the company, then I'm going to start a proxy fight, and I'll force you to sell it. That's the only way my fund can realize a satisfactory return from the stock."

This guy was used to seeing Internet companies bought and sold at high premiums. He thought that if we sold the company, the buyer (perhaps one of our biggest competitors) would pay a 25 percent premium and his investment's fund would make millions. As for how Boston Beer would fare afterward, this guy couldn't care less. He was stupid, too. He'd invested millions in Boston Beer and never took the time to understand our ownership structure.

I reminded my investor that if he had read our proxy statement, he would have discovered that he couldn't start a proxy fight or force a sale, since I owned all the voting shares. And I wasn't about to sell the company. "It's one thing to make threats," I told him, "it's another thing to be stupid. I can deal with people who make threats, but I don't know why I'm talking to someone so stupid."

I was *pissed*, both at his greed and at his assumption that I would cave in and compromise everything we had built. Greedy people are bad enough. Greedy, stupid people are intolerable.

In the end, he got the last laugh. After I blew him off, I heard that he planted a story in *Businessweek* that we were a takeover target for Miller Brewing. Our stock popped 20 percent and he dumped his shares at a nice profit. Once people figured out that the story was groundless, our stock went back down.

I learned an important lesson—that the value of the stock is not the same as the underlying value of the company. The stock goes up and down according to the whims and wiles of Wall Street. The value of the company depends on elements that contribute to the creation of real value—things like providing superior products at fair prices. You need to be learning and innovating, giving your people interesting, motivating work and compensating them fairly, creating value for your community, and doing it all in a way that yields a good profit. That's not what much of Wall Street values, but it's what creates long-term value for investors.

Never mistake the value of the stock for the value of the company. As I wrote earlier, a thousand-dollar investment in Boston Beer Company at the very beginning is now, more than thirty years later, worth over two million dollars. Not a bad long-term return for those with patience. It just goes to show that you really can grow as a company, even when on the surface it seems like you're just standing still.

34

ENDURE THE ENDINGS

SADLY, NOT ALL the amazing people who did so much to help launch Boston Beer Company would accompany us all thirty years. The most emotionally difficult departure of all was that of my business partner, Rhonda Kallman. I need to take a deep breath as I recount this story, because it's still painful for me all these years later to recall how I lost my partner and friend. Some things just suck and don't stop sucking. But there are lessons in the story, so here goes.

As our company moved through the A-B crisis, Rhonda continued to play a critical role running the sales force. She was deeply respected and revered the way good leaders are revered—that is, by everyone, most of all me. She was my friend and my closest confidant at the company, every bit the partner I had envisioned. In 1997, when our board asked me who I wanted to be CEO in case I got hit by a bus, I said "Rhonda." I deeply respected Martin Roper as a manager, but I saw Rhonda as the more inspirational leader at the time. With her unique talents, passion, and drive, she was the heart and soul of the company. Some of our board members and investors were uneasy with the notion of Rhonda as CEO, disqualifying her because of her lack of education and broader business experience. I acknowledged that she needed additional experience and training in many things a CEO deals with, such as operations, legal matters, or how to navigate a company's complex financial statements, but we could fix that. In fact, she was already enrolled in Harvard Business School's Executive Education program.

As ambitious, accomplished executives, both Rhonda and Martin were vital to the future of the company. I didn't favor one or the other; I saw that they had complementary skills and personalities. I envisioned the three of us working together to lead Boston Beer long into the future and counted them both as close friends. Although formal titles didn't mean all that much to me, I knew they were important to others, so as a sign of how equally I regarded our two top executives, I added marketing to Rhonda's portfolio, giving her formal oversight over half the company, while Martin got the other half, operations and finance. My role as the founder was to weave in and out everywhere, playing a part in areas where I could be of use as well as representing Boston Beer Company to the world. When people asked what I did, I told them I had two priorities, the quality of the beer and the culture of the company. Those were the only things I couldn't delegate to people who were better managers than I was.

My vision of the three of us leading Boston Beer proved short-lived. The board had asked me a theoretical question about succession, and I'd answered it under the assumption that I wouldn't be dying anytime soon. In 1998, however, I was starting to think more seriously about letting go of the CEO role and retaining only my formal chairman title. I had always known a day would come when I could delegate more. My father had told me that it usually takes a different person to run a company than it did to start it. An entrepreneur brings drive, innovation, raw energy, and the mentality of pushing boundaries. You never want to lose that as a company, but you also have to recognize that once a business reaches a certain size it needs someone with different talents and qualities making the decisions.

At $200 million in revenues, we had about reached that size. And I was tiring myself out. There was a lot of talk of craft beer being dead, and I was constantly traveling to work our local markets while also handling the responsibilities of CEO in Boston. I didn't want it all to go away, but I wanted to slow it down. Executives who leave say all the time that they want to spend more time with their families, and in my case it was true. By this time, Cynthia and I had two small girls, and I wanted to see them grow up. Meanwhile, with our brewery acquisition, the company was becoming more complicated to run; it would be better if we had a CEO who stayed primarily in Boston because I was continuing to travel a lot.

It was becoming apparent that Martin was succeeding with the brewery and was ready right now to become CEO. He was seasoned and had the full confidence of the board. Rhonda had the edge in terms of her longevity with the company and the passion she exuded to everyone, but I thought she needed broader exposure to other aspects of the company's management. Also, Martin made it clear that he was eager to lead a company. He would probably leave Boston Beer and find a CEO job elsewhere if we didn't name him to the position.

As the founder, I was responsible for the livelihoods of hundreds of people. I was starting to see that I needed to give Martin the title. I didn't like passing over Rhonda, but it was the right decision for the company. Rhonda thought she had earned the right to be CEO and was up to the task.

In retrospect, it should have been a pretty straightforward decision. Martin had the chops to be CEO at the moment, while Rhonda needed to expand her business acumen. So we needed a succession plan giving Martin the CEO reins for several years while Rhonda broadened her skills. At some point, Martin would succeed me as chairman, Rhonda would become CEO, and we would all live happily ever after as one big, well-managed company family. That's the arrangement I was on the verge of adopting, but sadly I didn't get a chance to implement it.

Rhonda's disappointment and pride caused her to make mistakes. At one board meeting in May of 1998, she and I were arguing about something, as we often did on our way to understanding each other and coming into agreement, and she stood up, announced that she was quitting the company, and walked out. Everyone present, including the five directors of our company, was astonished. We sat there for a while deliberating what to do. I knew Rhonda had lost perspective and didn't really mean to quit, but that didn't matter; you can't just say "I quit" at a board meeting of a public company unless you really mean it. It's a formal proceeding. Words have consequences.

Under different circumstances, I would have let Rhonda calm down for a couple of days before trying to patch things up, but I couldn't; she was an officer of the company, and legally we had twenty-four hours to issue a press release informing the market that she had resigned. I didn't want to see her go—I still very much believed in her—so I ran out of the meeting to get her. "Rhonda, do you realize what you just did?"

She shrugged. "I was mad at you; I was trying to get your attention."

"Are you crazy? You tried to get my attention? Rhonda, we share an *office*. You have my attention. You just severely damaged your credibility in front of the board of directors. Now I've got to patch that up. This is not good."

I did manage to smooth things over with the board, but after this incident I eventually concluded that Rhonda really did need more time to learn, especially with regard to working with a board, a prime responsibility of a CEO. I decided to make Martin president in late 1999 and then CEO in 2001. I planned for him to stick around for ten years in that role, by which time he would probably move on to a bigger company and Rhonda could get the top job. With this plan in place and all parties agreeable, we would have solved our succession dilemma for at least a couple of decades into the future.

When I told Rhonda in 1999 of my decision to make Martin

president and of my overall plan, I did the best I could to make it palatable. I promised we'd lay out an extended program of preparation for her, grooming her by having her run one of our brewing operations. "You know how much loyalty I have to you," I told her, "but this decision is not about you and me. It's about what's best for the three hundred people in this company who depend on us. Ten years from now, you'll be forty-eight and running a New York Stock Exchange company, and I'll help you get there." I reminded her that the three of us had already been dividing the leadership tasks informally among ourselves, and we would continue to do that; titles were not that important. Yes, she would technically report to Martin, but she could learn from him, we would still share an office like we always had, and in ten years she would have his job.

Rhonda quit soon thereafter, and I didn't see her for a year. The day she quit was the toughest day of my business career. Nothing I could say would make my decision work for her. She was convinced that she was ready to be CEO and that after almost fifteen years spent building the company from the bottom up, she had earned it. The break with the company was total; she sold virtually all her shares, more than a half-million shares at $7.50 a share and forfeited another couple hundred thousand options.

Years later, when we had patched up our differences, she revealed to me how betrayed she felt. "Jim, I would have taken a bullet for you, and you did that to me." But I was hurt, too. With her out of the picture, I now had to do her job for another five years, and I never got the time I wanted to spend with my family. It was a lose/lose situation.

Another thing Rhonda told me: "Jim, you only had two people to manage, and you screwed it up." In this, she was 100 percent right. I had screwed it up. Succession posed a difficult and obvious problem, and I should have spent more time looking for a way to resolve it that we all could live with. Probably I should have been more sensitive to Rhonda's understandable feelings about the public perception of her value and role, and I should have done more to emphasize how much authority she had as a lynchpin of the company.

Rhonda's departure hurt morale because she was so beloved in the company. We'll also never know what more we could have accomplished with her considerable talents. On the other hand, we managed to operate without significant disruption. Martin has done a more than excellent job as CEO, showing a sure hand as a manager and as a leader. As of 2015, he is still with us. As for Rhonda, she has gone on to start her own craft distillery on Boston Harbor and is presently distilling some of our beers into unique, multilayered whiskies. We're collaborating again, and having fun. It just goes to show: If you can endure the endings, you might eventually find that they're not endings at all, but rather the start of something new.

35

MIND YOUR PROTECTION

as our sales stayed level at about $200 mil-
lion, I never gave up on the idea of growth. There were occasional
moments of doubt when I thought, *Have we peaked? Will we ever grow
again? What if I am doomed to running a perpetually smaller company
every year, eventually having to lay people off?* But I never dwelled on
these thoughts. I believed that we had better beer and better people,
and that a new population of drinkers would eventually discover this
for themselves. How could Corona and Heineken be growing and not
Sam Adams? Our business had to turn around. Every problem has a
solution.

We continued to use our homespun radio ads with me talking to
drinkers as if I were in a bar with them. But these ads didn't seem to
be making much of a difference, so we partnered with a series of top
ad agencies to develop television campaigns. The work these agencies
produced was beautiful, the ads catchy and funny, but they didn't
move the needle on sales. I realized that we were just casting around,
looking for a magic bullet, without any rhyme or reason. Doing some
research and reading of my own, I came upon an approach to advertising I liked, one that involved rigorously testing potential ads with

audiences and only going with those that scored in the top 20 percent. We still hadn't produced a campaign that worked, but at least we were developing a solid framework for managing our annual ad budget, which by the early 2000s was in the millions.

Our experimentation during these years wasn't limited to advertising. We encouraged employees and executives to throw us ideas, and they did, including new products and promotional concepts. In establishing our direction, I sought to weed out the few worthwhile ideas from the seemingly hundreds of unfruitful ones. In the new products arena, we had some small, short-term successes entering beer and alcoholic beverage categories that were then hot. Twisted Tea was a good example. It might have seemed strange for a craft brewer of beer to create a novel beverage like hard tea; by the late 1990s, no other craft brewer had done it. But I prided myself on our willingness to branch out and try new product ideas as long as we remained within our core mission of offering the highest-quality products to the U.S. beer drinkers. Hard tea was actually less a leap than it seemed. We were already contract brewing the Tradewinds brand of nonalcoholic iced tea at our Cincinnati brewery. Hard tea had special challenges related to the fermentation, but like our beers, it used traditional ingredients, and we were also quite familiar with the intricacies of yeast. Making hard tea was something we could handle.

Our research with drinkers revealed that they were excited about the idea of a refreshing hard iced tea. We came up with a high-quality product that we liked and launched Twisted Tea in early 2000 as "BoDean's Twisted Tea," named after two guys who worked on it: Bo and Dean. We targeted it at more rural drinkers, the kind of people who drank Jack Daniel's. During hot summers on my grandmother's farm in rural southern Ohio, I had come to appreciate the "sweet tea" culture of the South. I used to bring a half-gallon Kool-Aid pitcher of sweet tea to a guy who worked at the next farm over; he'd keep it on his tractor and gulp it down to stay cool. BoDean's, I thought, would evoke the simple pleasures of spending time outside or whiling away a hot afternoon on the porch. As a company associated with New England, we would be broadening our geographic reach, and given that women liked tea as well, we would be building our business across gender, too.

It sounded great, but BoDean's Twisted Tea failed miserably. Granted, we didn't do much to support it—just some radio ads. We didn't win over many drinkers later in 2000 when a popular rock band called the BoDeans sued us for infringing on its name. We took "Bo-Deans" out of the name and relaunched the product as simply "Twisted Tea" in 2001. The head of the brand, Joe Whitney, was determined to make Twisted Tea a success. This turned out to be a good thing, as it gave us a chance to rethink the product. Twisted Tea didn't instantly restart growth for us, but over time it did develop into a solid, $200 million business. Seeing as few new brands ever reach that level of annual sales, it wasn't too shabby.

Sam Adams Light was a fairly similar story. By around 2000, I was resisting the idea of introducing another light beer; we had introduced one in 1987 called Boston Lightship, but it never really caught on and we phased it out in 1998. The lesson I drew from that experience was that light beer may not be consistent with the core Samuel Adams attributes of full-bodied flavor. Also, we had already succumbed to TV advertising, so I was reluctant to cross a second line— the launching of a light beer—that would bring us closer to the model of the big breweries. Yet by the turn of the century, light beer accounted for nearly half the beer on the U.S. market, and our distributors urged us to create one. I reluctantly came around to the realization that, yes, there were probably some light-beer drinkers out there who cared about full-bodied flavor, and some Sam Adams drinkers who patted their stomachs and said, "I wish I could drink more Sam, but I have to watch my weight." I came to agree with an industry observer who said that there's a bit of a disconnect for Samuel Adams to have a light beer, but it's sort of a necessity.

It took us two years and twenty-three test batches, but our brewers arrived at a light beer that offered great taste and complexity as well as fewer calories. Once I tasted Sam Adams Light, I was able to get behind it 100 percent. Miller Lite, Heineken Light, Bud Light, and Corona Light all had the same basic flavor profile, which was pale, crisp, and dry. Our light beer was none of those. It was malty, amber, and smooth—a really good beer that could stand on its own. Drinkers liked it in our initial tasting. A line on our back label read, "We did twenty-three test brews before we got it right, which means we poured twenty-two batches of pretty good beer down the drain." This prompted a visitor to our Boston brewery to remark, "I'd like to apply for a job as the drain."

We did well with the launch, holding kick-off parties in city after city with live music and thousands of people in attendance. Sam Adams Light made inroads for five years, but then, like Lightship, it saw its sales taper. My intuition was proven right: People who drink craft beer don't want light beer. When you're drinking a craft beer, you're not thinking about the calories any more than you are when you're eating Ben & Jerry's. Given the investment we made in advertising Sam Adams Light, we didn't turn much of a profit. Still, its launch energized our company, distributors, and retailers at a time of slow growth. We probably wouldn't have created a light beer if the company had been growing, but our higher-priority ideas weren't working.

In addition to product launches, we branched out in terms of the overall positioning of our brand. Since our biggest direct competitors— imported beers—were seeing upticks among younger drinkers and we weren't, we thought a change of positioning might help drinkers regard us as comparable to an import rather than as part of the "troubled" craft category. In 2000, we changed our tagline to "America's World Class Beer" and supported that claim by entering global beer competitions and playing up our awards. At the Australian Beer Festival in 1998, we took home "Best International Beer" and over twenty medals overall; we also won awards at the International Food Exhibition in London and the World Beer Cup in Brazil. The next year, we took home medals at the Monde Selection in Belgium and the Helsinki Beer Festival. To promote our standing among the world's finest beers, we held "liquid lunches" in nine U.S. cities, winning thirty-eight out of thirty-nine blind taste tests against leading imports like Heineken, Corona, Bass, and Guinness. Our Octoberfest seasonal beer became the first American Oktoberfest to be served in Munich, Germany, during Oktoberfest. In keeping with our desire to attract younger drinkers, we made it available exclusively at Munich's Planet Hollywood during the festivities.

We further supported our claim to be a world-class brewery by creating "extreme" brews that pushed the boundaries of what beer could be. Our efforts in this area had begun in 1993 with Triple Bock, which at 18 percent alcohol by volume was then the strongest commercially sold beer ever brewed. In 1999, we launched Millennium, which sold at $200 a bottle and was 20 percent alcohol by volume. In 2002, we took the art of brewing even higher with Utopias, a beer that set a new world record with 24 percent alcohol. As I told the media during the launch of Millennium, we weren't aiming to make a beer with a lot of alcohol; rather we sought to take beer to new heights so that people saw it as equal to wine and on the level of a Cognac, brandy, or port. The idea that a beer could cost $200 a bottle was simply unheard of then (and frankly, most people today still don't appreciate that as a possibility). But our extreme beers sold for far higher than that. In 1999, a college professor from Massachusetts bid $4,910 for Bottle Number One of Samuel Adams Millennium at a Yahoo! charity auction. Afterward, twenty more bottles were auctioned, garnering $1,500 each. We donated the money to the organization that had added so much richness to my life, Outward Bound.

We were also making a statement about our company, showing people that we might not have been the biggest or fastest-growing brewery in the world, but when it came to innovation and product quality, we were a leader. Brewing beers with this kind of alcohol content was a technical feat that nobody else had achieved; once alcohol content rises to a certain level, it kills the yeast that ferments the grain. For all of these products, we had developed a special strain of yeast that was more tolerant of alcohol.

If your company is struggling to grow, don't despair. Just keep trying new things. Some action is better than no action, and a small, temporary boost is better than no boost at all. You never know where your experiments will take you, and whom you'll meet along the way. It took all our energy during these years just to increase sales 1 or 2 percent a year and to prove that craft beer wasn't dead. We had to find a way to keep things working when they really weren't working.

Of course, be sure to take reasonable risks in your experimentation. None of our jabs at becoming a hot brand again via new products or advertising were "bet the company" moves made out of desperation. Since I retained all the voting shares of our stock, I didn't feel the same pressure many CEOs feel to take undue risks. All I needed to do was hold us steady and make enough incremental progress so that our distributors and other partners didn't abandon us. Despite my years climbing mountains, I wasn't personally inclined to take excessive risks, because the way I looked at it, I already had a great life: a wife I loved, four great kids, enough money to meet my family's needs, and a company that had far exceeded anything I had initially envisioned. I also remembered my fiasco trying to build a brewery in Boston—an instance when I almost did something foolhardy but pulled back just in time.

My decision-making process at Boston Beer was akin to the way an experienced climber scales a piece of rock. You climb ten feet, stick a piece of protection into a crack, clip into it, and climb another ten feet. If you fall, you only fall twenty feet, not a hundred. The principle is "only climb as high without protection as you're willing to fall." You can still take meaningful risks—just not any that are going to kill you. It might take you longer to advance, since you're climbing more cautiously. But that's okay. Mind your protection.

36

IF THE SUN IS SHINING, LOOK OUT FOR AN AVALANCHE

NO PROTECTION IN CLIMBING is foolproof. You can clip in all you want, but there are some risks you just can't avoid. The worst are the ones you can't see—those are the dangerous kinds. But a lot of things that look risky really aren't. Those are the scary kinds. At Outward Bound, we taught people to rappel off a cliff—you literally walk off a cliff backward into empty space. That scares the bejesus out of most people trying it, or even watching it, for the first time. In truth, that rope is strong enough to hold a car. But the first time you do it, it's pretty scary. It's just not very risky.

Other kinds of situations, however, really are dangerous even if they don't seem like it. Let's say it's a really beautiful early spring day. You're on the side of a mountain or glacier, walking across a sunlit slope that isn't too flat or too steep. You think everything is fine, but you're wrong. The sun is hitting the top layer of snow, causing some of it to melt. The water is trickling down into the layers of snow and ice below. When enough water hits a layer of less-dense snow that had fallen on top of an icy layer months ago, the entire layer begins to slide, and the snow breaks free. All of a sudden, you have an avalanche.

Not just an avalanche—*AN AVALANCHE!* These things can be hideously dangerous. People caught in avalanches tend not to survive. This is real danger, despite the bright sunlight and the sparkling snow.

In business, it's possible to survive avalanches, but it isn't easy. I know this firsthand because in 2002, an avalanche hit us and we survived—just barely.

It all started innocently enough. During the late 1990s, we promoted Samuel Adams by experimenting with media events and partnerships designed to appeal to our drinkers and draw media attention. In 1998, we held an event at Club Med on the Turks and Caicos Islands to launch our spring seasonal, White Ale. We invited dozens of radio jocks down to broadcast live. That event was so successful that we thought, *Hey, let's do this from Boston, from our brewery!*

That's what we did. We brought radio shows from top markets all over the U.S. to Boston for Grill and Groove (which we later renamed Summer Jam). It became a two-day summer festival of concerts featuring well-known bands like Smash Mouth, Train, Stone Temple Pilots, and G. Love & Special Sauce. We had all kinds of fun things going on, such as a Boston accent competition and a scale model of Fenway Park's Green Monster. Celebrities and semi-celebrities showed up for interviews with the jocks: Gene Simmons from Kiss, the Playboy Playmate of the Year, Johnny Knoxville, Matt Damon, Tara Reid, Mark Wahlberg, a Bill Clinton impersonator, and various other novelty acts. It was great fun for us and it gave us five or ten million radio listeners for two full days, building excitement around our beer among our core drinkers.

Another way we tried to snag younger radio listeners was by making regular appearances on radio programs, many of them "shock jock" shows. This was the heyday of shock radio. National and local personalities like Howard Stern, Opie and Anthony, Don Imus, and Bubba the Love Sponge were edgy, but they had mainstream success, becoming the highest-rated shows in virtually every market. They commanded the same audience we were targeting: educated, higher income, male—the kind of people who also went for the cheeky, semi-lewd, and anti-establishment humor of a magazine like *Maxim*. Other top food and beverage brands were going on these shows, eager for the unpaid radio exposure. Heineken had been a sponsor of Howard Stern for years. Budweiser, Miller, Snapple, Ford—they all sponsored these shows. It seemed safe. It wasn't scary, just dangerous.

Having long done radio shows and ads, I felt comfortable going on the shows, as they seemed to afford me a chance to convey substantial messages about our beer and create a conversation about craft beer in a funny, relevant way. The vast majority of the shows on any given day didn't cross that invisible line between acceptable and outrageous. The producers weren't asking me to do anything bad, like castrating a pig on air, as Bubba the Love Sponge allegedly did. I just had to talk about beer, drink the beer on air, and suffer the occasional joke about the "head" on Samuel Adams. I felt a bit like I was back in high school, the wise-ass kid who sat in back of the class cracking jokes. I didn't mind getting poked fun at; as we've always said inside Boston Beer, "We take the beer seriously, but not ourselves." And I marveled at the comedic talents of the radio personalities, their ability to come up with funny material instantly, day after day.

That invisible line got crossed, however, when Opie and Anthony, hosts of a popular show syndicated nationally through New York's WNEW-FM, orchestrated an outrageous and tasteless stunt. Opie and Anthony had shown up at our 2000 Summer Jam with the winners of a new contest they had held called "Sex for Sam." In the contest, which was then unknown to us, producers with cell phones accompanied couples to public places like Rockefeller Center, Carnegie Deli, or FAO Schwarz, where the couples got "points" for having sex. They could choose from a list of around twenty places with differing degrees of difficulty in which to earn points. The couple with the most points during the four-hour period of the contest won.

As far as radio antics went, this one didn't seem all that bad. So a couple may have had sex at our festival and a couple of people noticed. Big deal, I thought. Bad decision. Opie and Anthony began calling us the "Unofficial Sponsor" of the contest, and as we didn't field any complaints from drinkers or members of the public, we didn't stop them. The Opie and Anthony show was owned by Viacom, which also owned Nickelodeon, the children's channel. Viacom was paying Opie and Anthony millions of dollars a year, and over the years, the show had landed high-profile guests, so passively tolerating Sex for Sam seemed quite safe indeed. Bad decision again.

The next year during their Sex for Sam promotion, Opie and Anthony invited me to the studio but didn't tell me they were going to do the Sex for Sam thing again. Four or five couples started having sex right in front of us (this apparently was the starting gun, so to speak, of the contest). I was caught by surprise, not realizing that this was the day of the contest, but I didn't dissociate myself from Opie and Anthony, because I had become inured to the shock value; it seemed harmless to me. Another bad decision.

The third year of the stunt, I again came to the studio for the four-hour contest, whose big prize was a trip to our Summer Jam. This time, someone got the bright idea of including "Place of Worship" on the list of locations where couples could win points. Much to my chagrin, one couple from Virginia allegedly copulated in a dark corner at St. Patrick's Cathedral. A security guard saw the couple partially clothed, called the police, and had the contestants arrested. To add insult to injury, the Opie and Anthony employee who was with the couple referenced the child abuse scandals then gripping the church, saying something to the security guard along the lines of "Maybe meat-and-potatoes sex is what the church needs."

Oh. My. God.

I froze, not knowing what to do. I had a choice. I could play along, hoping that the story wouldn't blow up, or I could leave the studio. If I left, Opie and Anthony would certainly have singled me out for ridicule. Even in that moment, it seemed more scary than dangerous. So I stayed. More bad judgment.

The story of the arrest erupted in the New York tabloids, but mercifully Samuel Adams was not mentioned in the early days. The couple from Virginia was charged with obscenity, and the Federal Communications Commission launched an investigation of the incident. No one questioned why the prank was called "Sex for Sam." WNEW deflected critics by simply cancelling the show.

Ten days later, Samuel Adams and I were finally connected to the story. On Friday, August 23, the phone rang. It was a business reporter from the *Boston Herald*, the city's tabloid newspaper. He had been tipped off that I'd been in the studio.

A story ran on Saturday, but no other outlets seemed to pick it up. Could it be that we were home free? No such luck. On Monday, *The Boston Globe* called. From that point, the local and national media swarmed—reporters, producers, editors. We fielded calls from MSNBC, CNN, and local television stations and newspapers across the country.

The barrage of bad coverage lasted a couple of weeks, but we had bigger problems. The Catholic Church and many of its members were deeply and sincerely offended (as well they should have been). And a lot of bar and store owners are Catholic, particularly in the Irish parts of Boston and New York. The ex-mayor of Boston, Ray Flynn, once a Sam Adams supporter, was working to get people to start a boycott of our products. Some of them agreed. Flynn also appeared to be mobilizing other Catholic civic organizations.

The damage wasn't just happening in Boston but in New York, Chicago, San Francisco, and other cities across America with large Irish populations. Pictures were running in the media of bar owners pouring kegs of Samuel Adams down the drain. Email after email came into my inbox attacking me. One woman in Virginia wrote, "I will never buy your product, nor will anyone in my family. Grow up."

The owner of a popular Boston bar told an Irish newspaper, "This isn't a temporary boycott; this is a permanent 'throw out' of anything associated with [Boston Beer Company]." All this controversy was deeply embarrassing. I had made a series of bad decisions and jeopardized the company. On their own, none of them looked especially dangerous, but they all added up to one big disaster. How could I have been so stupid and insensitive?

For several months, my main job became calling and visiting bar owners, apologizing, and persuading them to accept my apologies. In all of my conversations, I didn't equivocate. I admitted I was wrong and sincerely sorry. I told them that I'd made a mistake. I had been in the studio, and I should have walked off the show. I made the wrong decision; I had learned my lesson and would never do anything like this again. My message seemed to get through. After two months, the anti–Sam Adams campaign had fizzled, and the crisis was over. We had survived.

We learned from the experience and were chastened; our cowboy days were over. No more shock jock appearances. If you screw up like this once, most people will forgive you. Screw up again, and it defines who you are.

Over time, we won back nearly all of the bars and restaurants that threw us out. In some measure, we learned who our friends were. As pained as I was by the angry messages, I was buoyed up by the support of friends, employees, and customers. If I hadn't held 100 percent of the voting stock, I would have been fired for sure. In the end, we lost one board member, but sales, much to my surprise, never dipped.

I learned just how easily an avalanche can sweep you down the mountain, even on the clearest and sunniest of days. When you've built up a successful business and have something to lose, like we did, it's vital to assess and understand the specific risks you face when making decisions. I've tried to remain constantly alert to the scary/dangerous distinction. You may shy away from some risks that are worth taking because they trigger irrational fears inside of you. In those situations, you should push yourself through the fear so it doesn't stand in your way. On the other hand, you need to stay alert to options that don't appear scary but really are dangerous. If you can't spot them, you're screwed; all you can do is try to dig your way out. Hopefully, you'll succeed.

37

THE RECALL: OUR BEST CRISIS EVER

DRINKERS SOMETIMES WRITE us, saying Samuel Adams isn't as good as it was when we first started. They think that as a company gets bigger, the quality of its products necessarily goes down. In our case, I know that isn't true. In fact, it's the opposite: As good as Samuel Adams was when we started, it's a much better beer than it was thirty years ago, because now we're able to exercise much more control over our ingredients and brewing process.

Other, more established craft beers have come in for criticism as well. In 2012, my friend Sam Calagione's Dogfish Head beers were bashed for being overrated and Sam himself was attacked for having a TV show about his brewing adventures. Now, I've known Sam a long time, and I've brewed beside him, so I know how innovative he is, and how committed he is to quality brewing. His beers are terrific—period. No true lover of craft beer should have a problem with his success. And because he has the energy and drive to get himself on television, he's done all craft brewers a service by promoting our shared passion. Succeed anyway.

Ultimately, growth presents entrepreneurial companies with a choice:

Improve the quality or lower the cost of production, fooling yourself into thinking that your lower-cost product is "just as good." For me the choice is clear. Good enough is never good enough when it comes to delivering superior quality. There is simply no resting place as a company grows. It's possible, even admirable, to grow beyond tiny *and* improve your quality.

When we bought noble hops during the early days, we had to take what the dealer offered. After I started making annual trips to Bavaria, I got better at inspecting the hops, rejecting batches of the flowers that seemed inferior. More important, I've developed relationships with preferred growers who, because of our scale, will harvest their crops exactly when we want them to maximize flavor. They will also process the hops to our exact specifications rather than for the general market.

Before packaging our hops for shipment to the United States, our Bavarian hop dealers freeze them to 40 degrees below zero, turn them into pellets, and vacuum seal them. This prevents the lupulin glands inside the hop flower (where all the wonderful oils and aromatics are) from rupturing, being exposed to air, and degrading. This proprietary process costs more, but given our scale and financial resources we can now afford to do it.

Our size allows for a similar higher quality in the malted barley we use. We have always bought the best barley on the market: two-row barley, which makes for a smoother, softer, creamier taste. As we've grown, we have been able to deal with one or two premier suppliers rather than many of them. This lets us tighten control over our barley's consistency. In addition, we developed a proprietary malting process that brings out the flavor we want for Boston Lager, making it smoother and richer. We couldn't deploy this special process when we were smaller because we were too small; in order to implement the process, our maltster has to stop production and set up its malt house just for us. With our scale, we can now afford this extra attention and care.

Beyond our ingredients, our enhanced stature as a "small" company allows us to respond more effectively to any unforeseen glitches that might occur in our production. Before bottles are filled, we put samples in front of a light box to look for foreign objects. It's an old-fashioned quality control measure called "candling the bottles." Most brewers don't do this, but we do. In late March 2008, the head of operations at our Cincinnati brewery called me, saying that they had picked up tiny pieces of glass, called "inclusions," at the bottom of a couple of bottles. We tested thousands more bottles to see if it was just a random occurrence or a problem with the entire shipment of bottles. We turned up several inclusions throughout the day's bottling run. Then we tested thousands more samples from other runs that were still in the warehouse—a few of those had inclusions too. And we checked beer from our Pennsylvania brewery. Yep, more inclusions.

Given that the inclusions were showing up everywhere, the problem obviously wasn't our bottling equipment. It had to be our glass bottles. Since we get glass bottles from multiple plants, we checked and determined that only one of our supplier's plants was shipping problem bottles. Fewer than 2 percent of bottles from this supplier were affected, but if you're putting out millions of bottles of beer a month, that's still a lot of bottles.

The question was: Did the inclusions even matter? I was surprised to learn that glass fragments below a certain size do not pose a threat to human health; you don't know you're swallowing them, and they go through your intestinal tract no problem, like the bits of sand that come with shellfish. The inclusions we found were almost certainly too small to pose any hazard. To make sure, I brought in former regulators from the Food and Drug Administration—the people responsible for food recalls—to see what they thought. They were on the fence. They advised me that we probably didn't need to do a full-fledged consumer recall of beer that had already been bought by drinkers; it was enough to just put a hold on the beer that was still in our distributors' warehouses and not ship any more out of our brewery.

They told me that this kind of thing happened all the time. Although they couldn't guarantee there wouldn't be any health issues, they said the risk was close to zero.

A consumer recall would be expensive for us and would also run the risk of alarming drinkers and impacting future sales. It could be the end of our business as we knew it if we permanently became known as "the beer with glass in it." We evaluated the situation on three criteria: public health, brand health, and financial health—in that order. I asked myself: If customers knew everything I knew, what would they want us to do? It was clear to me that they would want us to do a full recall. It was in our own self-interest, too, to do one. If we didn't recall the product, the story about inclusions would almost certainly get out anyway, making us look like a big corporation attempting the usual cover-up.

In the heat of the crisis, I held a conference call with our board to get its approval of the recall decision. The board members gave their blessing and hung up, leaving just my dad and me on the line. "So, Jim," he said, "now that it's just us, what do you think?"

"Dad, I don't know. I've never done anything like this before. We could lose everything."

Characteristically, my dad wasn't at all worried. "If we do lose everything, it's been a good ride." He paused for a moment. "Jim, I'm proud of you."

When we hung up, I felt good. Some crises a company faces, like the Opie and Anthony debacle, are self-inflicted. Some just happen, despite your best efforts to avoid them. But in either case, how you respond means everything. These are moments when your true colors really do shine through. In this case, we were going to do the right thing, and if our business tanked, so be it. It had been a good ride.

The recall cost $25 million to execute, much of a year's profits. Our entire company mobilized to make the recall happen and to manage publicity. We set up a call center and created a new Web site within seventy-two hours. Within a week, we got 25 million bottles of our beer back. There were 170 news stories the night of the recall on TV stations across the country, but after a few weeks, consumers forgot all about it. Sales only dipped a little. Ultimately, we only received one report of a very minor consumer injury throughout the entire episode.

We would not have been able to stomach the cost of a full recall if we weren't a company of a certain size. Certainly we wouldn't have been able to handle the recall as efficiently as we did. In fact, a much smaller craft brewer confided in me later that he had had a similar problem and just had to cross his fingers. If we were smaller, we might have done the same, rationalizing it by pointing to the advice of the ex–FDA officials.

I can understand why drinkers might automatically assume that our beer isn't as good as it used to be. That's how companies often behave when they reach maturity. Executives at these companies don't realize it, but they'll ultimately lose. If your company succeeds over the long term, it will be for one reason: because your products remain better than the competition's. If you're all about cutting costs as you grow, your product quality will suffer little by little, and eventually customers will notice the difference. They'll buy less of the product, regardless of how much money you pump into marketing. Over time, the choice to compromise quality will compromise your long-term performance.

If you ask me, people don't buy image. They buy the thing itself. Lose sight of that and you won't be growing for very long.

38

LET HELGA DO THE TALKING

IN THE WAKE of the Opie and Anthony episode, a writer castigated us in *Adweek* for our lack of marketing skills and unsuccessful outreach to drinkers, writing that Boston Beer had "long shown a flagrant and confounding disregard for patience and process with marketing and promotions. Unable to stay with a single agency or direction for any length of time, it has now stumbled on a ploy that has backfired big time." Not a few critics wondered if my hope of bringing back the craft brew revolution was a lost cause, and if I should sell the company. In September 2003, a *Businessweek* article wrote about my getting thrown out of a Manhattan supermarket for being overly aggressive with our point-of-sale material where I'd gone to make a sales call. "Will Jim Koch's beer ever be hip again?" I read that and was puzzled; we'd never been hip and hadn't tried. I wanted Samuel Adams to be different things, like passionate about brewing high-quality beer, innovative, and authentic. But not hip. And craft brewers in general seemed to feel this way. The ones who had tried to be hip succeeded for a while, and then went under when the hipsters moved on.

Ironically, Samuel Adams and the entire craft category would soon be growing again, not because market trends had fundamentally changed, but because after nearly ten years we had finally cracked the code and figured out how to communicate our core values to drinkers. We had come up with an advertising campaign that worked, a campaign that enabled us to make the most of our core values and integrity as the country's leading craft brewer. We had done what every struggling brand eventually needs to do to turn itself around: We stopped trying to do advertising and instead learned to tell our story. We had put aside the bullshit and gotten real.

The breakthrough came from yet more unorthodox moves born of experimentation. By 2001, I was so frustrated with conventional advertising agencies that I decided to bypass them altogether and hire two world-class creative talents, CJ Waldman and Marc Campana, to develop advertising for us. Believing that success in advertising was all about the creative, I figured we didn't need all the overhead an agency has, like account people, account planning, and so on. Applying the String Theory, I streamlined our ad budget, dispensing with extra overhead while paying for top creative talent to work on our business.

Marc and CJ's initial efforts for us in 2003 and 2004 included our "Always a Good Decision" campaign, which introduced a historical Sam Adams character into our ads. It was a little cheesy, and it didn't test in the top 20 percent—as our evolving approach to advertising required—but we ran it anyway as a temporary measure. The advertising did prove to be memorable, needling sales a bit higher.

In the spring of 2004, eager for new ideas that would work, we hired a bright guy named Tom Tominac and gave him a special initial assignment. "Tom, before we inculcate you in our conventional wisdom, which isn't working very well, we want you to immerse yourself in the real world and see if you can bring a fresh perspective to our business. For the first three months of your job, you don't have any responsibilities. Don't come into work. Just travel around, go to bars, talk to people, ride along with our salespeople, visit other breweries, and meet distributors. Listen to people, and stay away from market research reports!"

Being single, Tom was up for hanging out in bars for a few months. He came back to us with an interesting theory of how we were screwing up our marketing and advertising. "Here's the thing. We have all these great stories but we don't trust these stories enough to use them. We should tell people about the company and about our beer. People think we're a big company, part of Budweiser. They don't realize who we are and how we're different—how our products are different, the unique passion we have, the fact that our beer *is* better. We kind of lost track of that these past few years. If we tell them the real stories, they'll love it. We just have to talk about our company, our beer, and why we're proud."

Hmm, I thought, we hadn't been telling stories about ourselves lately at all. Putting the lens back on us and the great care we took with our beer would take us back to our earliest efforts to promote Samuel Adams—those radio and print ads that helped drinkers understand that all beers weren't alike and that a craft-brewed beer like ours offered better quality. It seemed so simple and so right.

We were having lunch at the time in a Boston restaurant. To test Tom's idea, I called the server over. "Do you have Sam Adams?" I asked.

She shook her head. "No, we don't carry them. They're too commercial, kind of like Budweiser."

I probed further. "Did you know Sam Adams has a brewery four miles from here? Did you know they have less than one percent of the market, and that the guy who started it first brewed it in his kitchen and is still with the company?"

"Really?" she said, dumbfounded. "I'll try that beer when I go out tonight."

Now Tom and I were staring at each other. *Holy shit!*

The question was: How do we start telling the story of us as a craft brewer again? At around this time, we had come up with the idea of shooting a video of the annual trip I take each year to Germany to hand-select the hops we plan to use. We would create a documentary showing people behind-the-scenes and put a DVD in our twelve-packs. By the time I had my lunch with Tom, CJ and Marc had already shot the video. When we reviewed it, we all immediately came to the same conclusion: This didn't have to be a special DVD. This could be a thirty-second spot that accomplished what Tom suggested—telling the story of our company to drinkers.

We edited the hops footage down to thirty seconds, and it was the first spot we'd ever made that tested in the top quintile for persuasiveness. During shooting, Marc and CJ had gotten some staged footage, like me going through the metal detector at the Munich airport with a beer opener in my pocket. None of that made it, just the authentic footage of me actually doing stuff. The final spot shows me explaining that hops are to beer what grapes are to wine. It shows farmers picking them and then me walking the hops fields and evaluating samples from the current crop. Helga, our hops dealer, comments that I don't just sniff the hops like most buyers do, but I dive into them to experience the full complexity of the scent.

That was the beginning of "Take Pride in Your Beer," a breakout campaign that would air for seven years, until 2012. Like the hops spot, the other spots in "Take Pride in Your Beer" educated drinkers about our beer and the virtues of craft brewing, with cut-ins of real people—me, Boston Beer employees, bartenders, and others—set against George Thorogood's gritty classic song "Who Do You Love?" We talked about the intricacies of how we brew, our ingredients, the high standards we employ, the unique characteristics of Boston Lager, and everything else that goes into making craft beers superior to the rest.

Helga was a matronly frau in her fifties. I think our initial spot with her was the only TV ad for beer that has ever had a woman in her fifties in it. That speaks to the radical nature of the concept. No longer were we mimicking others or modeling ourselves after beer advertising that had previously been done. Gone were the scripted stories, the meticulously planned lighting, the actors, the fancy graphics. Our new spots looked real because they *were* real. We had simply gone out there and shot footage, up to thirty hours per spot, editing it down through dozens of iterations until we had an amazing thirty-second mini-documentary. We weren't grasping at an angle we thought would work—a hook, a trend, a secret consumer insight. We weren't really doing "marketing" in the classical sense. We trusted that simply presenting our product and how we made it would be enough to attract drinkers.

When we began airing "Take Pride in Your Beer" in early 2005, our employees were energized. "Yes! Thank goodness!" they said. "These ads really do feel like us." Our sales went up within a month, and they have grown by double digits or near-double digits most years since. Between 2005 and 2014, our revenues grew from $238.3 million to $903.1 million and our stock price rose 1,160 percent, from $25.00 a share to over $200. The entire craft category has experienced renewed growth, with sales volume up 346 percent since 2005. Whereas in 2001 craft only comprised 3 percent of overall beer sales, in 2015 it snagged 11 percent. Between 2005 and 2015, approximately three thousand new craft breweries opened. And we became the leading voice for craft beer in the media, the only ones communicating the promise and potential of craft brewing on television.

I had long asked agencies to take the magic of our radio ads and translate it to TV. Instead, they had come back with fancy scripted ads and I had gone along with it, thinking that they were the experts. Our new ads were not only some of the most effective beer advertising out there, but they were far cheaper to make, costing one-tenth of normal beer ads. The lesson here, evident elsewhere in this book, is that sometimes the experts *don't* know best. Sometimes conventional wisdom *isn't* right. Sometimes what has worked in the past won't work for *you* and you need to develop an entirely new model. The only way to find out is to embark on a learning process, discovering what parts of conventional wisdom are wrong and eventually finding your own path. We were starting from scratch and making TV ads for a product—craft beer—that had never before been advertised on TV. When you're creating a new model such as we were, it takes time to develop the needed capabilities, beliefs, and practices. Sometimes, you have to fail and fail and fail and fail and fail and fail, and then you'll succeed.

"Take Pride in Your Beer" didn't single-handedly reignite the craft beer revolution. It played a role, but broader forces were at work, and I can't claim to know what they were. Still, "Take Pride" felt natural for us because we had been taking pride all along, even if drinkers or Wall Street hadn't noticed.

PART V

PACKAGING

Cans, bottles, kegs—there are many ways to present the finished beer to drinkers. The key is to do it in such a way as to protect what you've brewed, holding the ravages of time at bay for at least a little while until the beer can be enjoyed. To preserve a company you've built, you must develop new processes to do what you've always done, but to do it even better. And you must stay forever close to the spirit and love that got you started in the first place.

PRACTICE
FINGERSPITZENGEFÜHL

ONE OF THE GREATEST challenges any established business has is retaining the unique, inspiring culture it had as a start-up. The arrival of each new employee potentially erodes the culture because of his or her lack of familiarity with what you do and how you do it. If there's anyone who can reverse this process and plant the company's original values in new employees, it's you, the entrepreneur. And if there's one single most powerful moment in which to educate, it's that very first day of work, even the first morning. Everybody remembers their first day at a new job. The first day is the moment when new employees are most receptive to discovering important things about an organization. It's when they learn the culture. You need to wow your new hires, not bore them with forms and policies.

I spend five hours with new employees on their first day. One day each month, we start our new people on their weeklong orientation. During the first two hours of that first day, I talk to them about the company and its values. But my time with new hires has just started. I tell them we'll be doing something they probably haven't done since college. We'll have some pizza and then drink twenty-five beers. But we won't be downing a case of Natty Light or Milwaukee's Beast. These hires have graduated to mindful and intelligent drinking and will learn to appreciate beer, understand its ingredients, and identify specific flavors, all in two-ounce tasting cups. So at the end of the day, I come back and spend another three hours drinking with them. Of course, we have a whole training manual on how to taste beer, but I want to teach them myself how to do it, walking them through each beer, one by one, and pointing out the key flavors, talking about elements like mouthfeel, appearance, and aftertaste. I'll describe what flavors come from what ingredients, and what to look for in the beginning, middle, and end of a taste experience. Are the flavors in balance? Does one overpower another?

This beer tasting session usually goes until about 8 P.M., capping a twelve-hour day. It shows everyone that you can work long hours and still have fun. And I often get the best, most honest questions from new people while we're sharing those beers.

The concepts we go over this first day are just a preview of all that new people will learn over the course of the next week. At the end of this week, new people have to be able to give a tour at our brewery; even if we hired them as attorneys or accountants, we still expect them to have internalized the material enough to be able to stand in front of people and teach them about our company, its culture, and its products. That's how we know they are now the Boston Beer Company.

I also continue to spend time with employees as they make their way in the company, especially when they do things right. I try to congratulate employees for good work as much as I can; if I don't send two thank-you or congratulatory calls or emails a day, I feel like I've missed an opportunity. Most companies try to change behavior by telling people what they're doing wrong and what they need to improve. My experience has been that people usually know where they need improvement, and they improve faster when you point out what they're doing right. More good behavior then crowds out the undesirable behavior. And for me, it's a chance to reaffirm the importance of the mission, vision, and values we discussed way back in orientation.

A distributor once asked me why we spend so much time and money training people when they might just wind up leaving, and why I take so much of my own time up with it.

"What if you spend all that time and money training people and they leave?" he asked me.

On the face of it, the question makes sense. But I told the distributor he needed to think of it this way: What if you *don't* train people, and they stay? Isn't that much worse?

Passing the torch on to new cohorts of employees is only one of the ways I help keep our company on track as it passes its thirtieth birthday. I can't do everything, so I try to pick and choose to have the most impact. Across many areas of the business, I practice what the Germans call *fingerspitzengefühl*, or "fingertip touching." If you make a practice of getting out there and touching stuff with your fingertips, you can stay current and contribute while also providing the guidance a mature company needs.

Between 2005 and 2015, we saw significant growth as a company, but we still weren't by any means large compared to competitors like Anheuser-Busch or MillerCoors. The truth, however, was that we were certainly a bigger company than we used to be and big by craft industry standards, given that most of our community of brewers consists of neighborhood brewpubs or brewers that brew for their own zip code. In 2015, our volume surpassed 4 million barrels a year. To keep pace with demand, we invested millions upgrading our Cincinnati brewery, bought a new brewery in Breinigsville, Pennsylvania, and grew to more than thirteen hundred employees. The sale of Budweiser to the Belgian company InBev in 2007 and MillerCoors to SAB in South Africa made us the largest American-owned brewery, ahead of Yuengling.

To prevent us from becoming too "corporate," I make a point of sticking with the basics, continuing to engage personally with our sales team and customers. I still take many trips each month to local markets around the country, often getting up very early in the morning and getting to bed as late as 1 A.M. It is my way of showing by example that this is how we do it at Sam Adams—we get up earlier than everyone else, and we have a blast talking to our distributors and customers about the beer we love. A salesperson might come up to me and say, "Man, that was a long day!" And I'll say to him or her, "Yeah, but wasn't it a great day?"

I also have a hand in developing new and innovative partnerships. One of the favorites I've helped nurture over the years was Project Greenlight, with the actors Ben Affleck and Matt Damon. In the spirit of our Longshot home-brewing contest, we created a community of peer reviewers who submitted movie scripts online and evaluated others' scripts. A series of scripts were named finalists, and out of those, Ben, Matt, and their producer Chris Moore chose the winner. The first winning screenplay became a feature film starring Brian Dennehy, as well as an HBO special. Best of all, the winner, who was an insurance salesman in Chicago named Pete Jones, broke into Hollywood and has become a successful screenwriter. I've always believed that the line between a talented amateur and a practicing professional is arbitrary and can be erased by a lucky break. By "greenlighting the little guy," we affirmed our traditional commitment to nurturing the talents of people who have dreams and the courage to go for it.

I also practice *fingerspitzengefühl* by helping to innovate the experience of drinking our beers. In 2005, I asked Jean-Michel Valette, one of our directors, who is a Master of Wine, whether a glass can really affect the way a wine tastes. "Oh, absolutely," he told me. "You take the same bottle of wine and put it in six different glasses, and you'll taste the difference." So I did that, buying a bunch of Riedel glasses and using them to taste several wines and beers. Sure enough, the shape of the glass really did affect the flavor.

I had an idea: Let's develop the optimum glass for our Samuel Adams Boston Lager. I assembled a team of experts, including two Ph.D.s in sensory science; our brewers; and a glass manufacturer. For any glass we created, I wanted to know *scientifically* that it really optimized the taste. Many breweries put out their own glassware and it's just marketing; they don't pay much attention to whether the glass improves flavor. We tested every shape and size of glass, mug, and vase imaginable—maybe 120 or 130 in all. We discovered specific elements of the design of a glass that affected the taste of Samuel Adams and from there designed the Samuel Adams Lager Glass. Blind taste tests established that the glass really did improve flavor.

In 2007, after two years of development, we introduced our glass in the market. A pronounced rim around the top of the glass creates turbulence as the beer leaves the glass, releasing more flavor in the beer just as it hits your palate. The lip of the glass is wide, for your nose to get in there and really pick up the aroma. The lip of the glass turns outward so that the beer lands on the front of your palate. The classic pilsner glass shoots it to the back of your palate, which is good if it's a standard Bud Light or something. If you use a pilsner glass with Samuel Adams, you don't get the malty sweetness of the beer; all you get is the bitterness, the dryness, and the tongue sting from the carbonation.

We want drinkers to get the body and sweetness of the malt first and then the spiciness and bitterness of the hops. The shape and thickness of the glass allows your hand to warm the beer slightly; although our beer comes out of the average tap at 42 degrees Fahrenheit, we believe that 46 to 48 degrees is optimal for Samuel Adams Boston Lager. Finally, each glass has a laser-etched nucleation ring at the bottom that allows a little column of bubbles to come up, releasing aroma all the way to the bottom of the glass. This was the first beer glass designed by an American brewery to elevate the drinker's taste experience, and it triggered other brewers and manufacturers to design glassware for specific beer styles.

In 2013, we took the beer-drinking experience further, introducing a special new Samuel Adams can. Working with the design firm IDEO, Ball Corporation (the can manufacturer), and professional beer tasters, we spent two years and more than $1 million studying food and beverage packaging from every conceivable angle. With a curved neck and wider lid, our Samuel Adams can lets more aroma-laden air enter a drinker's nasal passages, enhancing the taste experience. (A little-known fact: Most of what we think we're tasting we're actually smelling.) The can opening is located slightly farther away from the edge of the lid, placing it closer to the drinker's nose to help accentuate the hop aromas. The lip on our can is slightly larger, a feature that puts liquid at the front of the drinker's palate so as to enhance perception of the malt's sweetness. Like our glass, the Sam Can has an hourglass ridge to create turbulence that "pushes flavor out of the beer."

The improvement in taste from the Sam Can is probably less pronounced than the improvement from the Samuel Adams glass, but to me even a slight improvement in the taste experience is worth effort and expense. In keeping with our commitment to the entire craft category, we have offered this technology to other craft brewers free of charge.

Fingerspitzengefühl is, in a sense, all about sharing. By imparting what I've learned to customers and employees, and by modeling a spirit of innovation and playfulness with beer, I help keep the company young—and myself, too.

40

STOP PAINTING AND START PARTNERING

DURING THE SUMMER of 2007, people in our office spent a day painting a community center in our South Boston neighborhood as part of our community involvement and social responsibility commitment. As we were leaving, everyone was feeling great about the good deed we'd done. Everyone except me. Something didn't feel right. We are a business, and a business is about creating value. On this day, we hadn't done that. We had probably spent $10,000 worth of good management time to do $2,000 worth of mediocre painting. We could do better. In our efforts to be socially responsible, we had taken the usual "feel good" approach, and in my mind, that wasn't good enough.

Writing a check to a worthy cause wasn't good enough either. If we did that, we would just be taking someone else's money—our shareholders'—and giving it to a charity that we deemed worthy. I was better off just giving back the money to shareholders and letting them decide how to spend it. The only way I could justify corporate philanthropic activity in my own mind was if we could add significant value in the process. Somehow, we needed to bring the same spirit of entrepreneurship, invention, and creativity that we bring to our economic mission to our social mission.

After a year spent trying to figure it out, we finally came up with a better idea. We decided to focus on partnering with young businesses to help them succeed. In batting around ideas, we realized that tiny start-ups often flounder not because they lack good ideas but because they lack certain missing pieces, such as expertise and financing. Thinking back to 1984, I wished I had been able to get a bank loan for my business instead of relying on friends and family. I also wished I had access to more nuts-and-bolts business advice. My Harvard education and management consulting experience hadn't prepared me to do a sales call, set up a payroll, design packaging, sign a decent real-estate lease, source obscure ingredients, or put together a successful PR effort. As an established company, we now had experts in all those areas working for us. So why not create a program that not merely helps deserving start-ups with funding but also gives them the coaching and advice they need to succeed?

In 2008, we launched Samuel Adams Brewing the American Dream, a program to help provide hardworking food, beverage, and hospitality business owners with the essential ingredients to start, strengthen, and grow their small businesses. Partnering with the microlender Accion, we offer small business loans (under $25,000) to small and up-and-coming businesses in the food and beverage industry. We also do speed-coaching sessions in the evenings that give entrepreneurs access to a couple dozen Boston Beer employees and local professionals who volunteer their expertise in specific areas. We screen participating companies for loans carefully, making sure they'll be able to use our money well to grow their business, create jobs, spur economic development, and eventually repay their loans. This isn't charity; we don't want entrepreneurs who will take out a loan and fail, because a failing business creates no jobs or economic development.

During the first seven years of the program, we extended more than six hundred loans totaling nearly $7 million, helping to create or retain 2,700 jobs—more than we have *inside* our company. Happily, more than 98 percent of the loans we made were repaid. Some four thousand companies have taken advantage of our speed-coaching sessions.

One business we helped through Samuel Adams Brewing the American Dream was a small, out-of-the-way deli in Boston called City Feed and Supply. With $12,000 from us, City Feed moved to a great new space on Centre Street in Jamaica Plain, a busy central artery, allowing the company to continue to employ its roughly twenty people and to add new employees. In another case, we loaned $4,000 to an entrepreneur who had a tiny cupcake store so she could also make frozen lemonade. The extra income from the lemonade added 20 percent to her gross receipts and let her hire two additional employees. We've funded and coached a woman who makes vegan cheesecakes, a guy who wanted to start a coffee roasting business, and a Jamaican take-out counter that wanted to expand—all kinds of unique and interesting businesses that just needed a little help to become something great.

Lucy Valena is an extremely passionate barista who launched a high-end coffee catering company with the idea of providing coffee for special events, gallery openings, dinner parties, and businesses. Her loan from our program went to pay for equipment such as commercial coffee grinders and an espresso machine. Almost two years later, the success of Lucy's catering venture enabled her to take the next step and open her first café.

Lucy opened a wildly successful café called Voltage Coffee & Art in Cambridge, followed by a second location in Boston. She saw a unique opportunity to amplify the local "coffee culture" by doing two things the high-end coffee chains weren't doing so well: delivering a really high-quality coffee and creating a community around the love of the bean.

Entrepreneurs are essentially artists of their craft. Lucy's challenge was to stop thinking solely like an artist and start adding in the business mind-set. Once she folded these two thoughts together, she was able to expand her business and pursue her passion. In fact, since she's been with the program, she's told us that she believes the training and technical support we offered were invaluable in changing the way she thinks when it comes to her business. All of this started with speed coaching and a $4,200 loan.

As part of Samuel Adams Brewing the American Dream, we've used our resources to help out fledgling competitors in our own industry. In 2011, we picked two start-up craft brewers—Roc Brewing Co. in Rochester, New York, and MateVeza, out of San Francisco, California—to participate in a more intense mentorship program. The entrepreneurs from these companies came to our brewery for two days of consultation with our employees. They could receive help with hops buying, label design, recruiting—whatever they wanted. These entrepreneurs were good people. Like me at the outset, they just wanted to create a nice, successful business for themselves, doing what they loved. We thought we could help them out and even though they were competitors, we were willing to do it. By the end of 2015, more than two dozen small brewers were participating in the Brewing the American Dream program, receiving loans, coaching, and mentoring from our team.

Partnering with start-up businesses inside and outside our industry is very much in our own self-interest because of the ways it affects our people. With Samuel Adams Brewing the American Dream, our employees have benefitted directly from the chance to interact and help start-up companies. Many established companies talk about becoming more entrepreneurial, but there are few better ways to get employees to think opportunistically than by enabling them to climb into the trenches with start-up companies and see the world from their points of view. As our employees have found, entrepreneurs are extremely energizing to be around!

As a general principle, established companies have an opportunity to behave like leaders and partner with up-and-comers in the industry. For an emerging industry to thrive, established companies within the industry can't just compete. They also can ensure that their fellow companies have a fighting chance. At times, that means setting aside considerations of profit and rendering aid, remembering once again what it was like to be tiny and vulnerable.

In 2008, we came to the aid of some of our smaller competitors, seeing a great opportunity to share our most valuable ingredient with them. Hop farmers not just in Germany but all over the world had experienced back to back years of bad crops. With global supplies reduced by 30 to 40 percent, many of the smaller craft brewers who didn't have preexisting contracts could only buy hops at exorbitant prices; many couldn't get hops at all. We were hearing stories about guys who had all their equipment in place and were ready to brew but could not make beer because they lacked hops.

Since we contract for our hops years in advance, we had more on hand than we needed for the year. We looked at our inventories and our needs, and we freed up forty thousand pounds of hops to sell to some two hundred brewers in need of hops. We did this by suspending production of one of our beers, the very hoppy Imperial Pilsner (interesting factoid: Imperial Pilsner requires twelve times the hops as Boston Lager). We sold these hops for what we originally paid for them, about $5 per pound, as opposed to the $30 a pound some dealers were demanding. One tiny brewer, Worth Brewing Company in Iowa, needed eighty-eight pounds of hops to get through the year, and we were able to make that happen. They're still in business today and growing. We asked brewers to request only as much hops as they truly needed, and virtually all of them complied. We couldn't help all the brewers who needed it—we didn't have adequate supplies—but we made an impact by helping several hundred. Of course, this has been easier for us since our industry already contains more than four thousand craft brewers. Helping dozens or even hundreds more to prosper doesn't change the competitive dynamics. And I've learned that the more people who benefit from your success, the more success you're likely to have.

41

WELCOME THE DUDE WITH THE GOLD-PAINTED TOENAILS

ESTABLISHED COMPANIES OFTEN struggle to innovate. They make packaging changes or line extensions and call it innovation. That's not enough. Just as established companies should stay close to the thing itself and improve product quality, so they can and should improve the creativity and curiosity that led to their success way back when they were small. Growing up as a company doesn't have to mean leaving behind entrepreneurship; you can actually get better at coming up with new ideas and bringing them to market.

The most important thing to do is establish an attitude within your culture of constantly soliciting fresh thinking. Good ideas can come from anywhere. They are like radio frequency signals coming in; you just have to be constantly looking. They might come from your sales force, from your production line, or even from outside the company. They very rarely come dressed for prime time, so to speak, so you have to accept the messiness to find the nuggets of gold.

In 2012, noticing how long it had taken us to bring an idea for a new beer to market (seven months), we decided to redesign how we tested and developed new recipe ideas. We created a nanobrewery in our Boston brewery capable of brewing beer in tiny, eight-gallon batches—in other words, a keg at a time. We hired a trained brewer, who was also an inquisitive home brewer, to run it. With our set-up, we can have thirty-two beers going at once. This dramatically increases the speed with which we can test and refine our products. Since we don't have to make big batches of any one new product, we can try all kinds of crazy concoctions and test every possible variety of a beer concept to see which tweaks make it taste best. We can even try brewing a number of varieties at once and blending them. We generate a lot of failures to get an occasional success.

Good ideas, I think, come from what's called "allopatric speciation"—in other words, semi-misfits, separated from the main population. You get the best ideas from people who in some way are out on the edge. My friend Alan Newman is one such guy. He helped found Magic Hat Brewing Company as well as the Seventh Generation brand of cleaning products and a business called Gardener's Supply Company—that's three nine-figure businesses. Alan lives up in Burlington, Vermont, and looks like a cross between a Hells Angel and a hippie love child, with a shaved head, a big bushy beard, and bright yellow glasses (although he might be into orange now). He wears sandals in Vermont in the winter and paints his toenails gold; he's on the edge in the way he does just about everything.

In 2010, I heard Alan got fired from Magic Hat (he had sold equity in the company and the money people realized Alan was unmanageable and fired him). I called him up and asked, "So, you got fired again?" He had once told me he'd been fired from every job he's ever had, including the first two companies he founded.

"Yeah, Jim. Story of my life."

"You have a noncompete, right? When does it expire?"

"Midnight on August 15th."

"What are you doing at 12:01 A.M. on August 16th?"

"I'm not staying up waiting for your freaking phone call. I'm gonna be asleep! Call me in the morning."

I did call him, because I knew Alan was a unique talent, and I could identify with the unmanageable part, so it didn't bother me. Alan happily accepted my proposal to become head of a new craft beer incubator within Boston Beer he called Alchemy & Science. It's located in Burlington, and basically it's Alan and his team dreaming up and pursuing new beer ideas. I told Alan that I wanted him to create five beer projects, each of which could grow to 100,000 barrels a year, and that we were willing to lose $25 million to get these brands off the ground. "I don't know what these brands are. We're working on our own new projects in-house, so I want you to get at angles of innovation we're missing. There's an infinite universe of beer out there. You're going to find one subset of that infinity, and we'll find another."

To get started, Alan worked on growing a downtown Los Angeles brewery he bought called Angel City Brewery. Angel City Brewery is perhaps the oldest brewery in Southern California, and he thought he'd be able to make it profitable again as Los Angeles' craft beer. Today, the brewery is up and running and doing a respectable business. At the same time, he designed a line of shandy-style beers under the umbrella the Traveler Beer Company. The tap handle design has a mustache with a hat on top. He forecast to us that shandys would be hot within three years. He was right. Since then, Alan has started similar local brewery projects in Miami with Concrete Beach, and New York with Coney Island.

Whether you have a dedicated innovation program or not, part of innovating is staying constantly alert to trends in the marketplace, including those that affect existing products. I mentioned earlier how our initial launch of a hard tea product, BoDean's Twisted Tea, failed, but a subsequent relaunch as simply Twisted Tea succeeded. The reason we decided to relaunch it was that we had been paying close attention to our markets, and we discovered that BoDean's was selling well in pockets of Maine, Michigan, and Montana. When we went up to Maine and talked to people, we discovered that the product was appealing to a whole different drinker than the one we initially had in mind for the relaunch. We thought upper-income twenty- and thirty-somethings would drink it, but in these locales blue-collar men had taken to it. These were not low-wage service workers or factory workers, but craftsmen who worked with their hands or had real skills—construction workers, cable TV repairmen, telephone line-men, plumbers, electricians. They made decent money on account of their skill, and they appreciated a refreshing tea beverage that was high quality and unique.

Relaunching a product that had failed twice was something we never would have done had we not been listening to customers and looking for patterns. Listening and looking led to an even bigger win with a different drink: cider. We had been in the hard cider business since 1995 when we started making hard cider and eventually launched HardCore, an English-style cider. (English ciders are traditionally a benchmark for good ciders.) The product did well for several years against our modest expectations, but it never caught hold in the market the way we would have liked, and over the years sales dwindled. We stuck with it for fifteen years because it had a small but loyal following, and we liked making it. In 2011, we started seeing an uptick in HardCore sales, even though we weren't doing anything different. We investigated and found that the winds had shifted. HardCore had sold to a younger demographic as something they could drink at home before going out for an evening of partying (an activity called "pregaming"). Now, a new source of demand had cropped up among craft beer drinkers who wanted a high-quality, traditional drink that tasted different from craft beer but could be consumed in a pint glass.

HardCore had been a traditional English cider—a working-class, rural drink with a slightly rough, sulphur taste. We created a new cider that departed from the traditional English cider taste and emphasized the intensity of the fruit. I worked with our cider maker to develop an entirely new cider from scratch, a cider we came to call Angry Orchard. Instead of using English apples, we would use apples from Normandy and northern Italy that were higher in the tannins and acidity that give an apple its strong flavor profile. We discovered that certain varieties of true cider apples, including Dabinett, Bisquet, and Bedan, made the best flavor and gave drinkers the sensation of biting into a fresh, crisp piece of fruit. We would sell it just as we would a craft beer, making it available at the same bars for about the same price as a craft beer.

We have never had a new product catch fire like Angry Orchard. In 2012 and 2013, the cider category experienced explosive growth, with many large breweries scrambling to put out their own ciders. It took us sixteen years to grow Samuel Adams Boston Lager to 10 million cases a year. Angry Orchard reached that in a little over two years' time, with women accounting for half the volume (a nice balancing of our predominantly male base of beer drinkers). As with our other products, we took a grassroots approach to selling it, winning over one bar or store at a time. That success, coupled with steady growth in our Samuel Adams and Twisted Tea brands, enabled our company overall to almost double in volume from 2009 to 2015. Not bad after twenty-five years.

Although growth is obviously a welcome development, hitting it big isn't the purpose of every experiment or innovation. One reason to experiment is of course to turn a profit, but another is simply because innovation is *fun* and doing the same thing every day is *boring*. Most entrepreneurs don't start companies because they want to become wealthy (or at least not solely or primarily for that reason). They start them because they want to control their own destinies and enjoy their daily work. What a shame when that spirit of fun becomes a casualty of success.

We have made some beers just for fun—for instance, Old Cock Ale. Have you heard of it? I didn't think so. I brewed it almost twenty years ago for my good friend and then–board member John Wing, who was turning fifty. Inspired by a medieval beer recipe for a "Bride

Ale" (a beer meant to help a young bride "fortify the resolve of her elderly bridegroom" on their wedding night), we took two freshly killed roosters and threw them in the brew kettle—feathers, feet, and all. The result was a brown ale with a slight brothlike character— pretty tasty. It was also slightly questionable, since rooster was not an approved ingredient in beer. But luckily, legendary U.S. Congressman Charlie Wilson (of *Charlie Wilson's War*) was at John's birthday party and he liked the beer. "Don't worry," he volunteered. "If those pissants at the BATF give you any trouble, you call me. I'll cut their appropriation." I have no idea if this was true, but John told me that Charlie had once cut a dozen airplanes out of the U.S. military's appropriation after they kicked Miss Universe, his girlfriend, out of the military transport that was flying them around Pakistan.

Brewing Hot Rock Beer was a different species of fun; think of that huge science experiment you dreamed up in middle school but never got to do. In the old days, brewers didn't have good ways of heating up the brew kettle without burning through the copper, so they would heat up rocks and dump them in the beer. We got several huge rocks, heated them to 2,200 degrees Fahrenheit in a pottery kiln across the street from our Boston brewery. Then, we used a forklift to dump them into the boiling wort. The result was a big sizzling mess, like putting dry ice into a skillet. The wort exploded and went everywhere, creating an interesting caramelization in the beer. Another old-style brown ale. Really tasty.

In 2006, we turned to American history for inspiration. We got George Washington's recipe for porter, Thomas Jefferson's recipe for a honey-lemon-ginger ale, and James Madison's recipe for a wheat and rye ale. To these we added a New England colonial root beer from Samuel Adams's day. These beers were all brewed in historically accurate ways. When smoking the malt, we used red oak from land that had once belonged to James Madison's estate. I'd be lying if I said these brews were the best-tasting liquids we'd ever created. Early in the process, we decided that we would make them as historically accurate as possible, even if that meant the beers were less drinkable. It was a commercial failure despite a nice write-up in *The New York Times*.

In about 2009, I got a call from Weihenstephan, the world's oldest brewery, wanting to know if we would collaborate with them on a new beer. Located in a village outside of Munich, Weihenstephan had been brewing beer since 1040. Today, the brewery is owned by the Bavarian government and is also a world famous brewing university and technical/research center. It's the place that had to assure the purity of Samuel Adams back in 1985 when we sought the imprimatur of the *Reinheitsgebot*.

We spent the next year or so working with Weihenstephan to create a Champagne-like beer, enlisting an upstate New York champagne maker to help us with some of the technical challenges, like the daily turning, or "riddling" of thousands of bottles. The Weihenstephan brewers were incredible partners. Every time we ran into a production problem, they brought in one of their professors, who was usually the world's expert in that specific area. We developed a special malting process that allowed us to make a unique malt for the beer. The result was Infinium, the first entirely new beer style in hundred years to have been created in Germany under the traditional beer purity laws.

We've also created new beers with other craft brewers. Sam Calagione of Dogfish Head Brewery called me one day and proposed that we work together to create an epistolary beer for an annual craft beer event called SAVOR. We did it old-school, handwriting letters back and forth to one another in which we planned out the beer. The result was a beer called Savor Flowers. Sam made a thousand gallons of rosewater in his brewery and shipped it up to us to use in the brewing process. As we stirred up the mash for this beer, the froth that formed on top (as often happens during this part of the process) formed into a perfect Tudor rose. It was so incredible that we took pictures of it. When I saw that, I thought, *Sam, God has blessed this beer!* In the end, we wound up collecting our letters and creating a little booklet of them that we hung around the neck of our bottles.

I've learned one important thing about successful innovation. I realized that all our successes begin as failures. My first batch of Samuel Adams exploded in my basement and peeled the wallpaper in my kitchen. Then it was turned down by five out of five wholesalers, and I had to take to the streets myself to launch it. Our first seasonal beer was Double Bock, another commercial failure but one that led to our seasonal program, now the largest seasonal program in craft beer. Twisted Tea failed as BoDean's Twisted Tea, then failed again as Twisted Tea, but we kept at it and it's been growing at double digits since 2002. HardCore Cider had been in decline for more than fifteen years and most companies would have killed it. But we had hope that someday there would be an opportunity to bring back hard cider, so we kept getting better at cider making. That failure lead to a rebirth of hard cider in America and a very successful new product, Angry Orchard Hard Cider. It's easy when something succeeds to forget the lesson that success usually comes into this world as a failure.

Remember that most of us came into this world as screaming, messy blobs of bad plumbing, but with a little love and attention and faith in our future, we managed to grow into fully functioning and successful human beings.

QUENCH YOUR OWN THIRST

I SOMETIMES WONDER what life would have been like if I had just accomplished what I'd envisioned in my original business plan and no more. I hoped to create a business with $1 million a year in sales and eight employees. What if the story had ended with a business that had never grown larger than that? Would I feel differently today about starting and growing a business?

I don't think so. Done right, business is a noble pursuit well worth our energy and passion. In business, you have to create value for other people before you can capture any value for yourself. You have to push yourself to learn and grow and to better yourself if you want to succeed. You quickly learn that the more others share in your success, the more success you'll have.

It's worthwhile asking yourself what you're getting out of your business, career, or job, beyond the money. When I launched the Boston Beer Company, I knew what I wanted: freedom, personal growth, connectedness with others, and the opportunity to do something that mattered, as least to me. I got all of those benefits long before I realized any financial returns. I have enjoyed the freedom of being my own boss, waking up every morning to decide what I need to do that day, stretching myself to learn new lessons or to find new capabilities. I have enjoyed spending time with people of every background and ability—from the first-generation immigrants who ran the convenience store in Manhattan where I made my first sale in that huge city, to the well-educated and well-heeled lawyers and bankers who handled our IPO, to all my amazing coworkers and fellow brewers. I've had a chance to give the world something simple that matters to me: a better glass of beer.

Whatever you do, don't quench someone else's thirst. Quench your own.

ACKNOWLEDGMENTS

Like brewing, writing a book is best when it's a collaborative effort. The idea of writing a book about my experiences starting and building Samuel Adams had been percolating for a decade. Then, three years ago, I started the process in earnest. When I talk to Sam Adams drinkers in bars and at our brewery, they always ask about the early days of the company. So, I made lists of stories and lessons that I thought would be educational and fun to read.

Let me start by thanking the core team at Boston Beer that supported me throughout the process. To Michelle Sullivan, Jessica Paar, Mike Andrews, John Dorman, and Ashley Leduc, I appreciate your patience with my handwriting (sorry I never learned to compose thoughts on a keyboard) and my unending need to polish, edit, and rewrite.

And to Fred Grein, the only corporate lawyer we've ever had (or needed). He incorporated the Boston Beer Company in 1984 and we've been his client ever since.

It was a pleasure to work with Seth Schulman, our contributing editor, who asked great questions and synthesized stories into chapters. His assistant, Christine Allen, and a former longtime employee of Boston Beer, Lucy Sholley, oversaw management of the transcripts and manuscript with dedication and intelligence.

Our agent, Jim Levine, gave us excellent direction and brought us to Flatiron Books, where we met our amazing editor, Will Schwalbe. He took an early draft of the manuscript and helped us understand how to make it a much stronger and more valuable book.

Thanks, too, to Mike Zimmerman, a magazine editor we have worked with over the years. He was the person three years ago who urged us to move forward with the book.

A constant presence in my life since 1984 has been my friend Sally Jackson. Her public relations agency helped launch Samuel Adams, and she continues to work with us today. She redefined "full service agency"; in 1992 she introduced me to my wife, Cynthia Fisher. And Sally was knee-deep in every aspect of the development of this book.

Writing this book took me away from family and friends for stretches of time, and I appreciate their understanding and hope they will find that the missed celebrations, activities, and dinners had a valuable purpose. I thank my children (in reverse order of appearance): Emily, Elizabeth, Charlie, and Megan. I have dedicated this book to my wife, Cynthia, but I need to thank her again specifically for everything she did to make this sometimes lonely writing process more pleasant. To my friend Rosabeth Moss Kanter, who has written so many wise business books, thank you for your insights into turning thoughts into a publishable book. And to Steve Leveen of Levenger for his further insights into the world of publishing. To my cofounder and dear friend, Rhonda Kallman, I loved sharing the early years of Boston Beer with you as my partner. You made it fun and you made it happen.

I was looking forward to sharing this book, as well as many years to come, with my best friend for thirty-two years, John Wing. Tragically, he died in July 2015, and I will miss his friendship, his advice, and his unending loyalty to Sam Adams.

Of course, without our Boston Beer family—colleagues past and present—none of these stories could be possible.

Where would I be without our drinkers, our wholesalers, and the establishments that sell our beers? You are the past, present, and future of Samuel Adams.

Cheers!

Jim Koch

JIM'S BOOKSHELF

There are more than enough good business books with solid, even inspiring, advice on how to do just about everything in business. I have compiled a different bookshelf here of books that are not in the ordinary run of business books but, nevertheless, taught me about business.

W. Edwards Deming, *Out of the Crisis.*
The father of the modern quality movement reminds us that mistakes and defects are rarely the results of the people who produced them and are almost always the results of the managers and the system the managers created. He also reminds us that genuine pride produces the great products that management through money or fear can never deliver.

Thomas S. Kuhn, *The Structure of Scientific Revolutions.*
The greatest philosopher of science in the twentieth century taught us that we don't really know what we know, because we apprehend the world through paradigms that structure our perceptions into models

that blind us to what's really true. And that most people in an industry or a discipline spend their time making small, incremental improvements to the existing dominant system, while occasionally someone, like Einstein or Copernicus, sees reality differently and creates a whole new structure for reality. And that new structure will in turn be superseded.

American Alpine Club, *Accidents in North American Mountaineering.*

This annual compilation describes and carefully dissects the year's serious and often fatal climbing accidents. Most fatalities begin as small mistakes that get compounded by unexpected conditions and bad judgment. There is usually a point where the right decision needs to be made and, if not made, fatality can only be avoided with unusually good luck (which rarely happens).

Joseph Campbell, *The Hero with a Thousand Faces.*

If you're going to undertake an enterprise, why not imagine it as heroic even if it's as mundane as starting a beer company. Campbell shows us how the gathering of internal resources is at the heart of all adventures and warns of the consequences for those who falter through pride and vanity.

Walter Isaacson, *Steve Jobs.*

A classic and inspiring story of the entrepreneur's journey where supreme confidence was eventually matched by humility and wisdom. Jobs's complete focus not on the product itself but on the consumer experience, from a single grand concept to the fanciest details, is unforgettable. Who doesn't love the tale of the creation of the first Mac, pirate flag and all?

Tom Hopkins, *Selling for Dummies.*

Selling is applied communication and vastly underrated in business education. If you want to know how viable your business is, go try to sell your product to some potential customers. This book is a solid primer on basic selling skills. You won't need much more.

Chris Argyris and Donald Schön, *Theory in Practice: Increasing Professional Effectiveness.*

Argyris was the original inspiration for the Fuck You Rule, although he developed it in academic jargon that nearly gave me brain damage. Argyris illuminates and dissects the reasons organizations fail to learn and why individuals are often smarter than organizations.

Nikki Giovanni, *Chasing Utopia: A Hybrid.*

A poet who showed that a truly beautiful beer, like a wonderful poem, has no reason to exist beyond our attraction to wonder and grace and that even the grandest of concepts find their existence in everyday objects like a bottle of Utopias.

Jorge Luis Borges, *Collected Fictions.*

The Argentine creator of magical realism in fiction who teaches us that there are compelling and logical alternatives to our familiar realities and that just slightly reimagining our everyday world can be a source of powerful insight and disturbing thoughts.

Guinness World Records, *The Guinness World Records.*

So familiar but rarely read as what it is: a compendium of human imagination, striving, and accomplishments great, comical, and even bizarre, sometimes from the great and talented but mostly from those, like the rest of us, who are ordinary and obsessed.

There are many fine beer books, but I've limited my list to the handful below that were written by some of the original brewers who helped create the craft beer revolution. I have found it a pleasure to read the way each tells his own story.

Sam Calagione, *Brewing Up a Business: Adventures in Beer from the Founder of Dogfish Head Craft Brewery.*

The founder of Dogfish Head Craft Brewery recounts his transition into brewing and his early days at it in the 1990s. He's a great brewer and a very good writer and storyteller.

Ken Grossman, *Beyond the Pale: The Story of Sierra Nevada Brewing Co.*

Sierra Nevada Brewing Co.'s cofounder talks about home brewing, scrounging for equipment, scaling up his brewery, and growing his business for thirty-five years.

Steve Hindy, *The Craft Beer Revolution: How a Band of Microbrewers Is Transforming the World's Favorite Drink.*

Steve tells the story of how a group of outsiders to the beer industry changed it forever. While I have disagreed with some of what Steve has written, it is still a great and passionate personal story told by one of craft brewing's most thoughtful and articulate figures.

Alan Newman and Stephen Morris, *High on Business: The Life, Times, and Lessons of a Serial Entrepreneur.*

This is the Dude with the Gold Toenails's story of his business adventures, including the Magic Hat Brewery. A lively and idiosyncratic story told with a smile.

Pete Slosberg, *Beer for Pete's Sake: The Wicked Adventures of a Brewing Maverick.*

Pete's Brewing Company with its flagship Wicked Ale was once America's second-largest craft brewery and is now largely forgotten. Unfortunately, Pete went from heart and soul of the company to a largely ceremonial role, as financial people neglected the company into oblivion.

Additional Reading

Tom Acitelli, *The Audacity of Hops: The History of America's Craft Beer Revolution.*

Bruce Aidells and Denis Kelly, *Real Beer and Good Eats: The Rebirth of America's Beer and Food Traditions.*

John K. Alexander, *Samuel Adams: America's Revolutionary Politician.*

John K. Alexander, *Samuel Adams: The Life of an American Revolutionary.*

Will Anderson, *Beer, New England: An Affectionate Look at Our Six States' Past and Present Brews and Breweries.*

Michael E. Cafferky, *Let Your Customers Do the Talking: 301+ Word-of-Mouth Marketing Tactics Guaranteed to Boost Profits.*

Kenneth C. Davis, *America's Hidden History.*

Stephen Denny, *Killing Giants: 10 Strategies to Topple the Goliath in Your Industry.*

Erving Goffman, *The Presentation of Self in Everyday Life.*

Steven D. Hales, *Beer & Philosophy: The Unexamined Beer Isn't Worth Drinking.*

Peter Hernon and Terry Ganey, *Under the Influence: The Unauthorized Story of the Anheuser-Busch Dynasty.*

Timothy Harper and Garrett Oliver, *The Good Beer Book: Brewing and Drinking Quality Ales and Lagers.*

Michael Jackson, *Michael Jackson's Beer Companion: The World's Great Beer Styles, Gastronomy, and Traditions.*

Peter LaFrance, *Beer Basics: A Quick and Easy Guide.*

Sean Lewis, *We Make Beer: Inside the Spirit and Artistry of America's Craft Brewers.*

Gordon MacKenzie, *Orbiting the Giant Hairball: A Corporate Fool's Guide to Surviving with Grace.*

Randy Mosher, *Tasting Beer: An Insider's Guide to the World's Greatest Drink.*

Marty Nachel and Steve Ettlinger, *Beer for Dummies.*

Daniel Okrent, *Last Call: The Rise and Fall of Prohibition.*

Garrett Oliver, *The Brewmaster's Table: Discovering the Pleasures of Real Beer with Real Food.*

John Porter, *All About Beer.*

Mark Puls, *Samuel Adams: Father of the American Revolution.*

Tom Robbins, *B Is for Beer.*

Bob Skilnik, *Beer & Food: An American History.*

Gregg Smith, *Beer: A History of Suds and Civilization from Mesopotamia to Microbreweries.*

Ira Stoll, *Samuel Adams: A Life.*

Philip Van Munching, *Beer Blast: The Inside Story of the Brewing Industry's Bizarre Battles for Your Money.*

NOTES

11 *womb with a view* Jim Koch, with Glenn Rifkin, "A Less-Is-More Lesson," *The New York Times*, July 20, 2003.

16 *my dad handed me an* Inc. *magazine article* Chris Hartman, "The Alchemist of Anchor Steam," *Inc.*, January 1, 1983.

18 *Reality is nothing but a collective hunch* Jane Wagner, *The Search for Signs of Intelligent Life in the Universe* (New York: Harper Perennial, 1991).

97 *I would smell a lawsuit coming* Mark Starr, "Beer Wars, Round Two," *Newsweek*, June 8, 1996.

99 *Jim Koch is the antichrist* Philip Van Munching, *Beer Blast: The Inside Story of the Brewing Industry's Bizarre Battles for Your Money* (New York: Random House, 1997), 166.

116 *the number of breweries and brands* Mimi Sheraton, "Roll Out the Barrel," *Time*, November 9, 1987.

117 The Boston Globe *regarded the controversy* Frederic M. Biddle, "Barroom Brawl: Tiny Brooklyn Brewer Takes On Boston's Sam Adams," *The Boston Globe*, May 6, 1993.

122 *less than 2 percent of the overall market* Lindsay Chaney, "New, Larger Set of Players Entering Craft Brewing Business," *Knight Ridder/Tribune Business News*, September 17, 1995.

123 *taking hold in the Pacific Northwest* Ibid.

123 *doesn't look like there is an end in sight yet* Quoted in Tim Goral, "Annual Microbrewery Report," *Modern Brewery Age*, May 10, 1993.

129 *$100,000 worth of beer a year* Peter V. K. Reid, "Jim Koch: Microbrewer," *Modern Brewery Age*, May 10, 1993.

129 *being a microbrewery* Ibid.

160 *$20 a share that institutional investors got* Numbers from Reed Abelson, "Boston Beer: The Sad Fall of an I.P.O. Open to All," *The New York Times*, November 24, 1996.

160 *a quarter of our total offering* Steve Kaufman, "Some Companies Are Selling IPOs to Individual Investors, Who Have Traditionally Been Shut Out," *The Chicago Tribune*, October 17, 1996.

161 *it was worth it* Ibid.

161 *available to individual investors* Quoted in Abelson, "Boston Beer."

161 *big Wall Street insiders* Jeff Sommer, "No Bitter Aftertaste from This Stock Offering," *The New York Times*, February 18, 2012.

166 *hard to consider Bud the king of beers* Mike Ivey, "'Stealth Breweries' Targeted Some Microbrew Labels Misleading," *The Capital Times*, February 23, 1996.

166 *his family's product is lousy* "With Beer Giants Streaming, Miller Ads Attack Microbrews," *Advertising Age*, March 10, 1997.

169 *an IPO open to all* Abelson, "Boston Beer."

169 *craft brewers had experienced sales declines* David Sharp, "Nation's Taste for Specialty Beers Flat," *The Columbian* (Vancouver, WA), May 12, 2000.

170 *still held our shares a year later* Abelson, "Boston Beer."

182 *numbered about three hundred* "Who's Who," *The Boston Globe*, May 20, 1997.

194 *infringing on its name* Chris Reidy, "Boston Beer Company Tests Product in Maine," *Knight Ridder/Tribune Business News*, July 24, 2001.

196 *we were a leader* "Koch to Sell His Millennium Beer for $200 a Bottle," *Modern Brewery Age*, October 18, 1999.

202 *Some of them agreed* Georgina Brennan, "St. Pat's Sex Prompts Beer Boycott," *Irish Voice*, September 3, 2002.

210 *backfired big time* David Gianatasio, "Party Foul," *Adweek*, September 2, 2002.

236 *a nice write-up in* The New York Times: Florence Fabricant, "Food Stuff; Life, Liberty and the Pursuit of Happiness, with an Ale Chaser," June 28, 2006.

INDEX

Adams, Samuel, 45–46
Adams, Scott, 145–46
adjuncts, 96–100
advertising
   with ad agencies, 44–45, 47,
     192–93
   "Always a Good Decision" campaign,
     211
   Anheuser-Busch campaign, 164–72
   against imported beer, 96–100
   radio ads, 95–97, 192, 199–203
   sales and, 68, 89
   "Take Pride in Your Beer" campaign,
     213–15
   Tominac and, 211–12
   in *Village Voice*, 134–35
Affleck, Ben, 222
Alchemy & Science, 232
allopatric speciation, 231
"Always a Good Decision" campaign,
   211
American beer, 16–17, 84
American Revolution, 45

Anchor Brewing Company, 16, 20,
   115–16
Angel City Brewery, 232
Angry Orchard, 5, 234
Anheuser-Busch, 2, 164–72
Argyris, Chris, 145
Atlas, 78–82
Australian Beer Festival, 195–96
avalanche, in business, 198–200

Barth, Peter, 170–72
Bavarian hops, 206
BBC. *See* Boston Beer Company
BCG. *See* Boston Consulting Group
Beck's, 96–99
Bernadette, Andy, 134–35
Better Business Bureau's National
   Advertising Division (NAD),
   168–69
boiling, 51
Boston Beer Company (BBC). *See also*
   specific employees; *specific topics*
   average salary at, 143

Boston Beer Company *(continued)*
  boycott against, and recovery, 202–3
  challenges, in getting business
    started, 16–17
  culture at, 138–40, 179–80
  customer base for, 32–33
  distribution and, 57–58, 78–82
  employment by, 5, 110–11, 113,
    149–55
  founding of, 1–4
  funding for, 25–26, 132–33
  going public, 4–5, 156–63
  growth of, 102–3, 110–13, 120–25,
    175–83, 192, 214
  hiring process by, 29–31, 149–55,
    219–20
  Hudepohl-Schoenling and, 178–81
  incorporation of, 25
  investors in, 25–28, 38, 132, 157,
    183–84
  IPO, 156–63
  legal troubles overcome, 97–100,
    104–5
  marketing for, 32–34, 111, 147–48,
    210–15
  new brewery for, 130–36
  partnerships in, 29–31, 32, 186–91
  revenues of, 5, 24, 110, 188, 214
  succession in, of CEO, 186–91
  women at, 150–51
Boston Consulting Group (BCG), 4,
  14, 24
bottle color, 16, 17
bottling, 206–8
boycott against, and recovery, 202–3
brand development, 147–48
Brewers Association, 118
brewery equipment, 39–40
brewmasters, 1–2
Brooklyn Brewery, 116–19

Burchfield, Michele, 137–38
burglary, 104–5
Burke, Eddie, 117
Busch, August, III, 165–66, 168,
  172
business
  avalanche in, 198–200
  customers and size of, 24–25
  ideas, 15–17, 230–31
  partnerships in, 29–32
  value of, 184–85, 238–39
business management
  during stagnation, 176
  string theory and, 62–63, 134,
    177–78
business plan, 2, 17
buying goods, 64–65

Calagione, Sam, 205, 236–37
Campana, Marc, 211, 213
cans, 223–24
career change, 9, 11–16
champagne, 236
Christo (artist), 158–59
Clarendon Wine Co., 105–6
climbing, 104–5, 198
Clinton, Bill, 122
communication, 144–48
community involvement, 225–29
competition, 115–19
complexity, 40–41
computers, 56, 58–59
consumption, 53–54
contract brewing, 26, 65, 116
  campaign against, 164–68
  with Hudepohl-Schoenling, 178
  with Pittsburgh Brewing Company,
    38–41
cooling, 51
Coors, Pete, 168

co-packaging, 26
craft beer industry, 4–5
    Anheuser-Busch campaign and,
        169–70
    growth of, 115–16, 122–24, 214
    handcrafted beer and, 84–85
    large commercial breweries in,
        123
Cranberry Lambic, 122
criticism, 116–19, 205–6
culture, 138–40, 179–80
customers
    BBC customer base, 32–33
    business size relating to, 24–25
    importance of, 64–65, 72–73
    listening to, 64–65, 74, 233

Damon, Matt, 222
Dateline NBC, 166–67
decoction mashing, 38–40
Dinehart, Steve, 123
disgruntled employee, 104–5
disorientation, 109–10
distribution
    with Atlas, 78–82
    BBC and, 57–58, 78–82
    sales relating to, 57–58, 78–82
    three tier system of, 78
doc-in-a-box, 15
Dogfish Head, 205, 236–37
Double Bock, 120–21, 237
draft quality audits, 177
Dukakis, Michael, 135–36

education, 11–12, 18–19, 68–69, 130
employment
    by BBC, 5, 110–11, 113, 149–55
    new hires, 219–21
    profile test, 153
entrepreneurship, 14–15, 187, 226–29

expertise, 35–42
extreme brews, 196–97

failure and success, 237
Fallows, James, 176
fermenting, 107
financial discipline, 55–57, 62
fingerspitzengefühl (fingertip touching),
        221–22, 224
Flynn, Ray, 202
forklifts, 67
foundry, 22–23
freshness dating, 126–29
Fuck You Rule, 146–48
funding, 25–26, 132–33

Gardener's Supply Company, 231
Gearon, Dan, 44–45
Gearon Hoffman Goransson, 44
German beer purity law, 3–4, 236
Germany, 93–94
Gianocostas, Dean, 102
glasses, 222–23
goals, 86
Golden Rule, 147
Goldstein, Leonard, 81
Goldstein, Lewis, 147
Great American Beer Festival, 90–92,
        116
greed, 183–85
Grinnell, Dave, 134–35
growth
    of BBC, 102–3, 110–13, 120–25,
        175–83, 192, 214
    of craft beer industry, 115–16,
        122–24, 214
    criticism relating to, 116–19,
        205–6
    innovation and, 233–34
    quality relating to, 205–6

Haffenreffer Brewery, 25–26, 130–31
Hahn, Kurt, 150
Hallertau noble hops, 170–72
Hambrecht, Bill, 159–60
handcrafted beer, 84–85. *See also* craft
    beer industry
Hansen, Chris, 166–67
hard cider, 233–34, 237
hard tea, 193–94, 232–33, 237
HardCore, 233–34
Harpoon, 164–65
Heineken, 87, 96–99
Hindy, Steve, 116–19
hiring, 29–31, 149–55, 219–20
home brewing, 16, 35–37
Hopkins, Tom, 59
hops, 170–72, 206, 229
Hot Rock Beer, 235
How to Master the Art of Selling
    (Hopkins), 59
Hudepohl-Schoenling, 178–81
Hutchinson, Gail, 46

imported beer, 16–17, 84, 86–88,
    96–100
improvisation, 67–71
inclusions, 206–9
incorporation, 25
Infinium, 236
initial public offering (IPO)
    of BBC, 156–63
    description of, 156–57
    investors in, 157–61
    press release on, 159–60
innovation, 192–97, 211, 230–36
investors
    in BBC, 25–28, 38, 132, 157,
        183–84
    in IPO, 157–61
IPO. *See* initial public offering

Jackson, Sally, 43–44, 90, 92–93, 97
Japanese manufacturing, 176
Jeanne-Claude (artist), 158–59
Jefferson, Thomas, 235
Jones, Pete, 222

Kallman, Rhonda, 4, 181–82
    background, 29–31
    beginning pay and salary, 55
    departure, from BBC, 186–91
    marketing plan by, 32–34
    partnership with, 29–31, 32,
        186–91
    in sales, 67–69
    success relating to, 112
Kappy's, 64
Katz, Francine, 166–67
Kautz, Jim, 58
kegging, 83–84
King, Henry, 119
Koch, Charles J., 1–4, 9–10, 16
Krueger, Rae, 99
Kuhn, Thomas, 19

labels, 46–47, 56–57
    for taps, 121–22
large commercial breweries, 123. *See
    also specific breweries*
leadership, 141–43
learning, 82–84, 130–36
legal troubles overcome, 97–100, 104–5
light beer, 194–95
Liquor Control Board, 105
listening, 64–65, 74, 83, 233
Longshot, 124–25
Louis Koch Lager, 44

Madison, James, 235
Magic Hat Brewing Company,
    231

marketing, 4
  for BBC, 32–34, 111, 147–48,
    210–15
  sales compared to, 49–50
  world-class tagline, 195–96
markets, 49
mashing, 7, 38–40
maturation, 173
Maytag, Fritz, 16, 115–16
mentors, 35–42, 228
mistakes, 130–36
Moore, Chris, 222
More Like Us (Fallows), 176
Mother Teresa, 119

NAD. *See* Better Business Bureau's
    National Advertising Division
naming
  by ad agencies, 44–45, 47
  Louis Koch Lager, 44
  New World Lager, 44, 46–48
  public relations and, 43–44
  Sacred Cod, 44–45
  of Samuel Adams, 43–48
new hires, 219–21
New World Lager, 44, 46–48
Newman, Alan, 231–32
Newsweek, 97

Old Cock Ale, 234–35
Opie and Anthony show, 200–202,
    210
Oregon Ale and Beer Company, 124,
    166
Oregon Brewers, 166
outliers, 19–20
Outward Bound, 12–13, 141–42,
    144–45, 149–50, 198
  string theory and, 53–55
overconfidence, 132–34

Owades, Joe, 37–42, 93
oxidation, 16

packaging, 217, 223–24
partnerships, 29–32, 186–91
payroll, 55
Pittsburgh Brewing Company, 38–41
possessions, 53–54
premium beer, 86–87
press kits, 90
press release, 92, 159–60
price, 22–23
problem solving, 9–11, 113
profile test, 153
profit, in buying goods, 64–65
Project Greenlight, 222
promotional materials, 69–70
Ptolemaic theory, 19
public relations, 43–44, 89–90, 94
publicity, 89–94, 95–100
  after "Sex for Sam," 200–203
  smear campaigns, 116–18, 164–72

quality
  control, 206–8
  draft quality audits, 177
  freshness dating and, 126–29
  growth relating, 205–6
  value and, 22–23

radio ads, 95–97, 192, 199–203
recall, 205–9
Reinheitsgebot, 3–4
revenue, 5, 24, 110, 188, 214
risk, 9, 13, 203–4
Roper, Martin, 181–82, 186, 188–91

Sacred Cod, 44–45
safety, 180–81
salaries, 55, 130, 143

sales
  advertising and, 68, 89
  best sales call, 75–77
  distribution relating to, 57–58, 78–82
  dominant images in, 57
  education relating to, 68–69
  fear of, 57–61
  first, 59–62, 66–67
  golden rule of, 72–74
  How to Master the Art of Selling, 59
  Kallman in, 67–69
  marketing compared to, 49–50
  pitch, 59–60, 68–69
  promotional materials, 69–70
  relationships, 72–74
  selectivity in, 73–74
  strategies, 58
  table tents for, 69–70
  techniques, 59
  value and, 49–50
"Sam to Standards" program, 177
Samuel Adams, 4–5
  Boston Ale, 122
  Boston Lager, 40–48, 90–92, 234
  Boston Lightship, 194
  Brewing the American Dream
    program, 226–29
  cans, 223–24
  Cream Stout, 122
  in Germany, 93–94
  glasses for, 222–23
  in Great American Beer Festival,
    90–92
  label of, 46–47, 56–57
  Light, 194–95
  Millennium, 196
  naming of, 43–48
  Triple Bock, 196
  White Ale, 199
Savor Flowers, 236–37

Scheurle, Walter, 97–99
scientific revolution, 18–19
seasonal beer, 120–22
selecting customers, 73–74
Seventh Generation, 231
"Sex for Sam," 200–203
shelf placement, 70
small-scale beer company, 2–3
smear campaigns, 116–18, 164–72
Snyder, Arthur F. F., 27
social responsibility, 225–26
speaking up, 144–48
St. Pauli Girl, 96–99
stale beer, 126–29
Starr, Mark, 97
stock
  IPO, of BBC, 156–63
  value of, 184–85
stomach ulcers, 20
string theory
  business management and, 62–63,
    134, 177–78
  financial discipline and, 55–57, 62
  maintaining, 56–63
  Outward Bound and, 53–55
  success relating to, 112–14
  in travel, 63
success
  culture relating to, 139–40, 179–80
  Kallman relating to, 112
  rules for, 22–23
  string theory relating to, 112–14
succession, 186–91
sugar, 38–39
Summer Jam, 199–201

table tents, 69–70
Tagamet, 20
"Take Pride in Your Beer" campaign,
  213–15

tap labels, 121–22
teamwork, 141–43
telecommunications, 15
Thaler, George, 93
Tominac, Tom, 211–13
training, 219–21
travel, 63
Traveler Beer Company, 232
trespassing charges dropped, 104–5
Twisted Tea, 193–94, 232–33,
  237

UPC barcodes, 121–22

Valena, Lucy, 227–28
Valette, Jean-Michel, 222
value
  of business, 184–85, 238–39
  price and, 22–23
  quality and, 22–23
  sales and, 49–50
  stock, 184–85
Van Munching, Philip, 99
Village Voice, 134–35

visibility, 70
Vonnegut, Kurt, 53

Waldman, CJ, 211, 213
Warner, Andrea, 151
Washington, George, 235
Watson, James, 18
wealth, 53–54
Weihenstephan, 236
White, Jeff, 180
White House, 101–2
Whitney, Joe, 194
wholesalers, 25, 78, 127–29
Williams, Colleen Keegan, 137–38, 152
Wing, John, 133, 167–68
Wm. S. Newman Brewing Co., 134
women, 150–51
world-class tagline, 195–96
wort, 51
Worth Brewing Company, 229

yeast, 38–39

Zucker, Jeannie, 102, 103–5

ABOUT THE AUTHOR

Jim Koch is the founder of The Boston Beer Company and brewer of Samuel Adams. He founded the company in 1984, using his great-great-grandfather's recipe and set to the task of revolutionizing American beer. Samuel Adams Boston Lager has been an important catalyst in the American craft beer revolution for more than thirty years, bringing full-flavored, award-winning beer to the American beer landscape. The Boston Beer Company has become one of the leading American craft breweries and now accounts for just over one percent of the U.S. beer market. Jim and his family reside in Newton, Massachusetts, home of the Fig Newton.